CONGRESSIONAL POLICIES, PRACTICES AND PROCEDURES

SEPARATION OF POWERS IN THE FEDERAL GOVERNMENT

OVERVIEW AND PERSPECTIVES

Congressional Policies, Practices and Procedures

Additional books in this series can be found on Nova's website under the Series tab.

Additional e-books in this series can be found on Nova's website under the eBooks tab.

CONGRESSIONAL POLICIES, PRACTICES AND PROCEDURES

SEPARATION OF POWERS IN THE FEDERAL GOVERNMENT

OVERVIEW AND PERSPECTIVES

JOSEPHINE SPENCER
EDITOR

NOVINKA

New York

Library of Congress Cataloging-in-Publication Data

ISBN: 978-1-63485-189-3

Published by Nova Science Publishers, Inc. † New York

CONTENTS

PREFACE

Congress's role and operation in national politics is fundamentally shaped by the design and structure of the governing institution in the Constitution. One of the key principles of the Constitution is separation of powers. The doctrine is rooted in a political philosophy that aims to keep power from consolidating in any single person or entity, and a key goal of the framers of the Constitution was to establish a governing system that diffused and divided power. These objectives were achieved institutionally through the design of the Constitution. The legislative, executive, and judicial branches of the government were assigned distinct and limited roles under the Constitution, and required to be comprised of different political actors. The constitutional structure does not, however, insulate the branches from each other. While the design of the Constitution aims, through separation, to prevent the centralization of power, it also seeks the same objective through diffusion. Thus, most powers granted under the Constitution are not unilateral for any one branch; instead they overlap. This book provides an overview of separation of powers. It reviews the philosophical and political origins of the doctrine; surveys the structure of separation of power in the Constitution; discusses the consequences of the system, for both the institutions and for individual political actors; and provides a discussion of separation of powers in the context of contemporary politics.

In: Separation of Powers …
Editor: Josephine Spencer

ISBN: 978-1-63485-189-3

Chapter 1

SEPARATION OF POWERS: AN OVERVIEW*

Matthew E. Glassman

SUMMARY

Congress's role and operation in national politics is fundamentally shaped by the design and structure of the governing institution in the Constitution. One of the key principles of the Constitution is separation of powers. The doctrine is rooted in a political philosophy that aims to keep power from consolidating in any single person or entity, and a key goal of the framers of the Constitution was to establish a governing system that diffused and divided power. These objectives were achieved institutionally through the design of the Constitution. The legislative, executive, and judicial branches of the government were assigned distinct and limited roles under the Constitution, and required to be comprised of different political actors. The constitutional structure does not, however, insulate the branches from each other. While the design of the Constitution aims, through separation, to prevent the centralization of power, it also seeks the same objective through diffusion. Thus, most powers granted under the Constitution are not unilateral for any one branch; instead they overlap.

The constitutional structure of separation of powers invites conflict between the branches, particularly between Congress and the President. The electoral structure of the federal government provides not only

* This is an edited, reformatted and augmented version of a Congressional Research Service publication R44334, prepared for Members and Committees of Congress, dated January 8, 2016.

separate bases of authority, but also *different* bases of authority for political actors, as well as different time horizons. Likewise, the assignment of powers under the Constitution is not only overlapping, but also somewhat vague, creating inter-branch contests for power across many key functions of the government. Finally, numerous questions of authority are not even addressed by the Constitution.

Although each branch has strong incentives to protect its prerogatives, in many cases individual political actors have incentives that run counter to their institutional affiliation. In particular, political actors will often, quite reasonably, place the short-term achievement of substantive policy goals ahead of the long-term preservation of institutional power for their branch of government. Likewise, partisan or ideological affiliations will at times place political actors at cross purposes, where they will be forced to choose between those affiliations and their branch affiliation. Such anti-branch incentives are important contours to consider for political actors seeking to increase the power of their own branch.

The problem of institutional power coming into conflict with other goals is particularly acute for Congress, especially in relation to the executive branch. As individual members of a large body, Representatives and Senators may not believe they have the responsibility or the capacity to defend the institution. Those who may feel such responsibility, such as party and chamber leaders, will often find themselves in situations in which policy or party goals, either their own personal ones or those of their caucus, come into direct conflict with institutional goals. Even when Congress does choose to institutionally defend itself, it often finds itself speaking with less than a unified voice, as only the most vital institutional powers have the ability to unify Congress.

This report provides an overview of separation of powers. It first reviews the philosophical and political origins of the doctrine. Then it surveys the structure of separation of power in the Constitution. It next discusses the consequences of the system, for both the institutions and for individual political actors. Finally, there is a discussion of separation of powers in the context of contemporary politics.

INTRODUCTION

Congress's role and operation in national politics is fundamentally shaped by the design and structure of the governing institutions in the Constitution. One of the key principles of the Constitution is separation of powers. The doctrine is rooted in a political philosophy that aims to keep power from consolidating in any single person or entity, and a key goal of the framers of the Constitution was to establish a governing system that diffused and divided power. Experience with the consolidated power of King George III had led them to believe that "the accumulation of legislative, executive, and judicial powers in the same hands ... [was] the very definition of tyranny." [1]

These objectives were achieved institutionally through the constitutional separation of powers. The legislative, executive, and judicial branches of the government were assigned distinct and limited roles under the Constitution, and required to be comprised of different political actors. The elected branches have separate, independent bases of authority, and specific safeguards prevent any of the branches from gaining undue influence over another.

The constitutional structure does not, however, insulate the branches from each other. While the design of the Constitution aims to prevent the centralization of power through separation, it also seeks the same objective through diffusion. Thus, most powers granted under the Constitution are not unilateral for any one branch; instead they overlap. The President has the power to veto legislation; the Senate must approve executive and judicial nominations made by the President; the judiciary has the power to review actions of Congress or the President; and Congress may, by supermajority, remove judges or the President from power.

This report provides an overview of separation of powers. It first reviews the philosophical and political origins of the doctrine. Then it surveys the structure of separation of power in the Constitution. It next discusses the consequences of the system, for both the institutions and for individual political actors. Finally, there is a discussion of separation of powers in the context of contemporary politics.

The American System in Global Context

The American system of separation of powers is not the most common arrangement of democratic institutions in the modern world. Most modern democracies are parliamentary systems, in which the legislative branch is sovereign, and the executive has no independent constitutional base of authority, instead being chosen by the legislature.[2] Indeed, even when the United States has participated in the construction of democratic governments in the 20th and 21st centuries—in Germany and Japan after World War II; in Iraq in the first decade of the 21st century—the chosen structure has been parliamentary, not an American system of separated powers.

This is perhaps, in part, because experience has suggested mass democracy and legislative supremacy—two (at the time) untested concepts that concerned the framers of the U.S. Constitution in the 18th century—to be satisfactory arrangements for stable democratic governing. There is also a widely held contemporary belief that modern democracy is inherently based on political parties and that parliamentary systems produce stronger parties.[3] Neither of those prospects would have sat well with the framers of the American Constitution, who were skeptical of political parties.

Finally, parliamentary systems are often encouraged for fledgling democracies because they tend to produce unified governments that can relatively easily legislate and implement policy without difficulty, allowing for smoother government functioning during the dangerous and unstable early stages of a new national governing system.[4] At their core, parliamentary systems are based on contested elections followed by unified party control of the powers of government. This is quite emphatically not the case with the American system. Our constitutional system is based on contested elections followed by separated control of the powers of governing. The system, by design, produces conflict.

Conflict by Design

The constitutional structure of separation of powers invites conflict between the branches, particularly between Congress and the President.[5] The electoral structure of the federal government provides not only separate bases of authority, but also *different* bases of authority for political actors, as well as different time horizons. Likewise, the assignment of powers under the Constitution is not only overlapping, but also somewhat vague, creating inter-branch contests for power across many key functions of the government. Finally, numerous questions of authority are not even addressed by the Constitution.

Although each branch has strong incentives to protect its prerogatives, in many cases individual political actors have incentives that run counter to their institutional affiliation. In particular, political actors will often, quite reasonably, place the short-term achievement of substantive policy goals ahead of the long-term preservation of institutional power for their branch of government. Likewise, partisan or ideological affiliations will place political actors at cross purposes, where they will be forced to choose between those affiliations and their branch affiliation. Such anti-branch incentives are important contours to consider for political actors seeking to increase the power of their own branch.

Separation of Powers: Origins

In order to fully illuminate the contemporary implications of our separation of powers system, it is helpful to understand its origins. The structure of the Constitution reflects the collective preferences of the state delegates who drafted it in 1787. These preferences were chiefly shaped by two things: the political philosophy of the colonial Americans, and their actual political experiences as English colonists. The fingerprints of both can be found throughout the legislative debate at the constitutional convention, the arguments for and against the Constitution during the ratification debate in the states, and, of course, in the text of the Constitution itself. Undoubtedly, the colonists' philosophy also shaped how they understood their colonial interactions with London, and vice versa, making it difficult if not impossible to untangle the degree to which either had primacy in shaping the Constitution. What is clear, however, is that by 1787, the philosophy and the experiences of the framers had created something of a consensus among them about how an optimal government should be structured.[6]

Philosophical Roots

The political theory underlying the constitutional separation of powers goes back thousands of years, and traces its development through many eminent philosophers, among them Aristotle, Aquinas, Machiavelli, Locke, and Montesquieu. Virtually all of these philosophers were living under non-democratic systems of government, or systems of very limited democracy that did not feature separation of powers. Therefore, much of their writing is either normative—what should such a system look like?—or applied to non-democratic governing structures. As a result, much of the development of the philosophy ignored the practical problems of establishing a separation of powers democracy, and by the time of the American Revolution, left the framers long on theory but short on practical advice.

Functions of Government

The conceptual roots of separation of powers are usually attributed to ancient Greek and Roman writers. Aristotle is typically credited with articulating the first conception of government as divided into three basic functions or "powers," which he labeled "deliberative," "magisterial," and "judicial," and which roughly correspond to the contemporary notions of legislative, executive, and judicial roles of government.[7] The ancient philosophers, however, did not conceptualize the possibility of (or benefit of) separating these functions among different officials or institutions. In both Athens and Rome, the various functions were often taken on by single entities.[8]

Later philosophers tied this concept of functions to the idea of a "mixed government," in which the interests of society would be balanced through the use of multiple forms of government.[9] This formed the basis of pre-modern English government for centuries: a hereditary monarchy, limited in its authority by a legislature consisting of elements of aristocracy (House of Lords) and democracy (House of Commons). While the "mixed government" system did not separate functions by institution, it did promote the idea that liberty for all could be enhanced by blocking any individual or entity from dominating government. Since these classes of society were rigid, their interest were perpetual and often in conflict. By combining them in the various forms into the government, none would gain the power necessary to dominate the others.

Enlightenment Thought

The modern conception of separation of powers developed largely among 17th and 18th century Enlightenment thinkers. Although many writers were active in this area, John Locke and Montesquieu are usually given credit for articulating the philosophy. In the *Second Treatise on Government*, Locke argues that a division between the legislative and executive powers is fundamentally necessary to secure the liberty of the people. If the two functions are fused into a single person or entity, the likely result is tyranny. Locke also explains the concept of a "mixed government," in which multiple forms of governing—monarchy, oligarchy, democracy—are simultaneously used.[10]

The fully formed conception of separation of powers as understood by the framers of the Constitution is credited to Montesquieu. In *The Spirit of Laws*, Montesquieu identifies three powers of the government: legislative, executive, and judiciary. He then argues for their placement in the hands of different people or entities:

> When the legislative and executive power are united in the same person, or in the same body of magistrates, there can be no liberty, because apprehensions may arise, lest the monarch or Senate should enact tyrannical laws, to execute them in a tyrannical manner.
>
> Again there is no liberty, if the judiciary power be not separated from the legislative and executive. Were it joined with the legislative, the life and liberty of the subject would be exposed to arbitrary control, for the judge would then be the legislator. Were it joined to the executive power, the judge might behave with violence and oppression.
>
> There would be an end of every thing, were the same man, or the same body, whether of the nobles or the people, to exercise those three powers, that of enacting laws, that of executing the public resolutions, and of trying the causes of individuals.[11]

Montesquieu also provides the basis for the concept of checks and balances, writing that the executive power and legislative power should be "restrained" by each other.[12] For Montesquieu, the critical executive restraint on the legislature is the veto; the "power of rejecting" legislation. The critical restraint of the legislature is the annual power of the purse, for if "the executive power [were] to determine the raising of public money ... liberty would be at an end."[13]

At the heart of the theory is a simple proposition about human nature: as noted by James Madison, men are not angels, and left unrestrained they will tend to abuse power.[14] To leave one man as both lawmaker and judge, for Locke, was to invite tyranny. Drawing on the Aristotelian description of the various "functions" of government, Montesquieu envisioned a government structure that would preclude the tyrannical combinations, by isolating what he saw as the three prime functions: making laws, executing laws, and trying alleged lawbreakers.[15]

Colonial Experiences

It is unclear to what degree these philosophies influenced colonial thinking in the late 18th century. What is not unclear is how the structure of colonial governance provided ample reason for the colonists to become wary of the consolidation of power. Experience with the consolidated power of King George III had led them to believe that "the accumulation of legislative, executive, and judicial powers in the same hands ... [was] the very definition of tyranny."[16] Experience with the royal governors of the colonies led them to distrust institutions that had mixed government functions. And experience with legislative democracy in the fledgling states during the 1780's had reinforced their concerns about the potential for "elective despotism."[17]

Colonial Government

The majority of the colonies in North America were run by "mixed governments," much like the central British government.[18] Eligible colonists were allowed to elect representatives to the lower chamber of an assembly, but the governor was appointed by the crown, and in addition to the executive duties, had significant influence across the other functions of government. The royal governor typically had absolute veto over colonial statutes, appointment authority for the upper chamber of the legislature (called the "governor's council"), and the power to dissolve the assembly.[19] The governor's council also typically served as the highest court in the colony. The assembly did have some checks on the governor—most notably control over his salary and authority over taxation.[20]

This arrangement served the colonists fairly well during most of the 18th century. The indifference of parliament and the crown toward the administration of government in the colonies resulted in a political culture that was much more democratic in character than the culture in England proper.[21] Having developed a norm of self-government during the first half of the 18th century, the tighter control over colonial government exhibited by parliament and the crown after the conclusion of the French and Indian War caused significant tension between the colonists and British government.[22] When the colonists sought to address these problems, they found that the institutions of the colonial governments were not well-suited to successfully challenging the crown once the crown was intent on an active approach to colonial administration.[23]

Revolutionary Grievances

Once the crown took a greater interest in the administration of colonial government, the democratic character of the colonial governments receded and the power of the governors, and the direct power of the crown, under the system became apparent.[24] In common thought about the American Revolution, much is made about the lack of representation of the colonies in the English parliament.[25] Even a cursory reading of the Declaration of Independence, however, reveals that most of the particular grievances of the colonists revolved around the administration of government within the colonies, and that many of those grievances were framed as problems with the fusion of government functions under the crown.

For example, the list of facts provided in the Declaration includes the following charges against the king:

- He has dissolved Representative Houses repeatedly;
- He has refused for a long time, after such dissolutions, to cause others to be elected;
- He has called together legislative bodies at places unusual, uncomfortable, and distant;
- He has refused to Assent to laws ... for the public good; and
- He has made Judges dependent on his Will alone, for their tenure and ...salaries.

These specific grievances suggest a developing colonial belief that the separation of powers was a prerequisite for a government that sought to preserve liberty, and that the centralization of such powers would necessarily lead to oppression and tyranny.

Early American Challenges

Following independence, the newly independent states began to pursue governmental structures more closely aligned with our modern view of the separation of powers. Between 1776 and 1780, all 13 original states drafted new state constitutions. The colonial and revolutionary experience, however, also took on a strong anti-executive character. The colonial assemblies, after all, had been the branch of government controlled by the colonists and their principal source of governmental power. The dissatisfaction with the king and the colonial governors led many colonists in the 1770s to believe that strong legislatures were the key feature of optimal governments.[26]

Early on, in 1776 and 1777, many of the new states adopted new systems of government with weak and dependent executive branches.[27] In Delaware, Virginia, and New Jersey, the governor would be appointed by the legislature and had no veto or appointment authority.[28] In Pennsylvania, there would be no single executive; a council chosen by the legislature would take on the role.[29] Likewise, the national government under the Articles of Confederation contained no independent executive or judicial branch, instead leaving the creation of those functions up to the national legislature.[30]

Other states, however, adopted constitutions featuring separation of powers more in line with the future federal Constitution. The New York constitution of 1776 provided for an independent, elected governor with a three-year term, veto power, and appointment authority.[31] The Massachusetts constitution (1780) required that "the legislative department shall never exercise the executive and judicial powers... the executive shall never exercise the legislative and judicial powers ... the judicial shall never exercise the legislative and executive powers ... "[32]

By the early 1780s, many began to rethink investing so much power in the legislatures. Both Thomas Jefferson and John Adams were early opponents of the legislative-dominated state constitutions.[33] The experiences of Pennsylvania and other states with weak executives proved to be disappointing.[34] The failure of the Articles of Confederation as a national governing document further eroded belief in government by legislature alone.[35]

The Framers in Context

By the time the framers met to amend the Articles of Confederation, public opinion in the colonies had followed a meandering path, largely rejecting both the tyranny of an unchecked executive and the tyranny of an unchecked legislature. The proper arrangement of government for the enhancement of liberty is thus, they believed, one in which no one can gain unilateral power, and no power goes unchecked. As Madison argued in the *Federalist Papers*, the objective of the framers was to preclude a "faction" from gaining monopoly control of the government.[36]

The framers viewed human nature as inherently bad, and suspected that the natural inclination of men is to abuse power. Tyranny, to them, was "the accumulation of all powers, legislative, executive, and judiciary, in the same hands."[37] To separate the functions of government into independent branches was necessary but not sufficient. Each branch would also need the ability to stand as a check against the others. No branch, however, would possess an overruling influence over the others, and each would be provided with the necessary means to resist encroachment from the others.[38]

SEPARATION OF POWERS: STRUCTURE

Translating the collective political philosophy of the founders and their constituents into a government required the construction of institutional structures that reflected and, hopefully, sustained their preferences. Institutional design of the new Constitution, therefore, required careful consideration. The legislative, executive, and judicial branches of the government were assigned distinct and limited roles under the Constitution, and political actors are restricted from serving simultaneously in the legislature and another branch. The elected branches have separate, independent bases of authority, and specific safeguards were designed to prevent any of the branches from gaining undue influence over another. Although not constitutionally guaranteed, longstanding norms also now exist that provide each branch with its own independent resources for staffing, research, and advice.

The following section discusses four key aspects of the constitutional separation of powers: separate roles and authorities; separate personnel; independent electoral bases; and separate institutional supports. It then discusses the checks and balances placed with the various separate institutions.

Separate Institutions

The legislative, executive, and judicial branches of the government are each given separate constitutional bases of power. The executive and legislative branches are populated by leaders who are drawn from different constituencies on different electoral timetables. And judicial branch actors, while not elected, are insulated by tenure provisions that require supermajorities to remove them from office.

Distinct Roles and Authority

The Constitution divides the federal government according to its core functions—legislative, executive, and judicial—and places each function primarily in a separate institution. The three institutions are given their distinct authority of their function, made plain by the first sentences of each of the first three Articles. Article I begins, "All legislative power herein granted, shall be vested in a Congress of the United states."[39] Article II begins, "The executive power shall be vested in a President of the United States of America."[40] Article III begins, "The Judicial power shall be vested in one supreme Court[.]"[41] This is separation of powers, as understood by the founders, in the most basic sense: the President is authorized to execute the law; the Congress is authorized to make the law; and the Court is authorized to judge the law.

Separate Personnel

The Constitution specifically prohibits individuals from serving in Congress and another branch of the federal government. Article I, Section 6 states that "[N]o Person holding any Office under the United States shall be a Member of either House [of Congress] during his Continuance in Office."[42] While this guarantees that no one will simultaneously hold position in Congress and one of the two other branches, the Constitution places a further prohibition on Members of Congress serving in any office which was created during the period for which they were elected, or for which the salary was increased.[43]

Independent Electoral Bases

The elected officials of the legislative and executive branches—the President, Vice President, Senators, and Representatives—are all drawn from constituencies that do not normally involve the other branches. The President and Vice President are chosen by electors from the states, all of whom are themselves currently chosen by popular vote in the states, but are by law picked in the manner each state legislature directs.[44] Members of Congress are specifically barred from being electors, guaranteeing that they have no direct influence in the election of the President or Vice President.[45] Members of the House and Senate are chosen by direct election in their districts and states, respectively, with no input from the other branches of the federal government.[46]

While the federal judiciary is not filled in an independent manner—judges are nominated by the President and confirmed for office by the Senate—the Constitution mitigates legislative or executive branch intrusion into the judiciary by providing federal judges with tenure "during good Behavior," which in practice amounts to life tenure.[47]

Independent Resources and Support

Each branch of the federal government has developed its own support structure of professional staff. Although not guaranteed in the Constitution to any branch—Congress has authorized and continues to fund the support structures and can, in theory, remove them—strong norms exist among both political actors and citizens that each branch of government should have the resources to fulfill its duties under the Constitution. The resources provide information and advice, conduct research and analysis, investigate problems, organize activities, and carry out other assignments for their principals.

Members of Congress have personal staff, as well as committee staff and chamber-wide and branch-wide support organizations to call on for support in the development of legislation.[48] The President has several thousand staff in the Executive Office of the President, and can draw on Cabinet officials or agency heads, who can in turn call on resources within the executive departments themselves.[49] The federal judiciary has both chamber staff to assist them as well as centralized staff in the Administrative Office of the United States Courts and several branch-wide support organizations.[50]

The Constitution prevents Congress from specifically reducing salaries of the executive and judicial branch. Article II prohibits the adjustment of the President's salary during his current term of office.[51] Likewise, Article III prohibits the reduction of compensation of federal judges during their service.[52]

Checks and Balances

While the Constitution provides separate institutions and bases of power, the structure does not insulate the branches from each other. While the design of the Constitution aims to prevent the centralization of power through separation, it also seeks the same objective through diffusion. Thus, most powers granted under the Constitution are not unilateral for any one branch; instead they overlap. The President has the power to veto legislation; Senate approval is required for executive and judicial nominations made by the President; the judiciary has the power to review actions of Congress or the President; and Congress may, through impeachment, remove the President, Vice President, and other "civil Officers of the United States." As political scientist Richard Neustadt has observed, what the Constitution created was "separate institutions sharing each other's power."[53]

Overlapping Responsibility

Although each branch is the primary actor in the function that corresponds to its institution, no branch has unilateral control over its core function. Congress is vested with the legislative power, but the President may veto legislation—ensuring him/her a bargaining position on legislation in most cases—and has the power to call the Congress into session.[54] The Supreme

Court, through the implied power of judicial review, may declare acts of Congress and executive actions unconstitutional.[55] The President is vested with the executive power, but Congress has legislative control over the bureaucratic design of the executive branch and the amount of financial resources the departments of the executive branch receive.[56] Finally, while the Supreme Court has the judicial authority, Congress has the authority to create the inferior federal Courts and prescribe their jurisdiction and regulations, as well as to refine legislation in response to judicial decisions.[57]

Appointment and Removal Authority

The constitutional system for filling both the offices of the executive branch and most of the federal judiciary requires the cooperation of both the executive and legislative branches. Principal officers of the United States, including federal judges and high-ranking executive officials are nominated exclusively by the President, but require confirmation by the Senate.[58] Under the 25th amendment, vacancies in the Vice Presidency are also filled through nomination by the President and confirmation by both the House and Senate.[59]

Although the President retains general removal authority over most executive branch officials, Congress has the authority to remove the President, Vice President, and "civil officers of the United States" (including federal judges) for treason, bribery, and other high crimes and misdemeanors.[60] The power, however, is divided between the House of Representatives, which has the power to impeach, and the Senate, which is responsible for trying those impeached by the House. This power is exclusive to Congress; there is no corresponding mechanism in the other branches for the removal of Representatives or Senators, which reveals the primacy of Congress under the Constitution. The House and Senate may expel their own Members, but no outside power, save elections, can otherwise remove them, reflecting the Framer's concept of the sovereignty of the people.

Investigations

Both the executive and legislative branches have investigatory authority over each other. The executive branch, subject to certain constitutional limitations,[61] investigates criminal conduct by Members of the House and Senate, and legislators suspected of violating the law can be prosecuted in federal court.[62] Congress has the authority to investigate activities in the executive and judicial branches, and these investigations can be the basis for either future criminal prosecutions or impeachment proceedings. In addition,

Congress has the authority to conduct routine oversight of executive departments to inform future legislation and resource decisions.[63]

War and Foreign Policy

The Constitution specifically divides matters of war and foreign policy between the branches. The President is commander in chief of the armed forces under Article II,[64] but Congress is granted the authority to declare war, raise and support an army and navy, and make rules governing the armed forces.[65] Congress also has authority over appropriations, including funding for any war effort.[66] The courts have the authority to declare actions of Congress or the President in relation to war unconstitutional.

General intercourse with other nations is also a shared responsibility. The President has many of the responsibilities of head of state, but the Senate provides its advice and consent to treaties, and Congress controls the appropriations and legislation needed to implement them.[67] In other cases, Congress or the President may often find ways to reach agreements without a treaty, either through bilateral agreements of the executive branch, or, in the case of Congress, through public law.[68]

SEPARATION OF POWERS: CONSEQUENCES

The constitutional structure of separation of powers is directly consequential for the practice of American politics. It incentivizes specific strategies and behaviors of both individual political actors and the branches of the federal government as a whole. This section discusses three broad consequences of the separation of powers: the inevitability of conflict in the American political system; the desire of each of the branches, in aggregate, to increase its relative institutional power; and the cross-pressures faced by individual political actors as they balance the accumulation and maintenance of power for their institution with policy or other goals that are often at cross purpose with such accumulation.

Conflict

The constitutional structure of separation of powers generates strong political conflict. With political actors in each branch having preferences over public policy but not the capacity to unilaterally realize those preferences, it is inevitable that disagreement will be constant and political actors will seek to expand the power and influence of their respective branches. Far from a defect of the system, this conflict is the very essence of the framers' goal: arrange the federal government such that no faction can accumulate enough power to singularly dominate.[69]

The source of conflict in the constitutional structure, however, goes beyond the basic separation of power. If the only structural differences between the branches were the authorities assigned to them and the preferences of the political actors, American politics would likely have much less conflict than it has traditionally exhibited. The Constitution, however, provides several other mechanisms that enhance conflict and limit the ability of any faction from gaining coordinated control of the functions of government.

Separate Bases of Authority, but Also Different Bases of Authority

While the elected branches of the federal government have independent electoral bases (i.e., neither branch has a primary role in choosing the members of the other branch), they also have *structurally different* electoral bases. Representatives are elected every two years, from districts drawn to be approximately the same size.[70] Senators are elected every six years on staggered terms, from statewide votes.[71] The President is elected every four years, from a national vote aggregated through state elections to an electoral college.[72] At any given point in time, the House, Senate, and presidency will be filled with elected political actors drawn from different constituencies at different points in time. No single federal election in the United States can completely alter the political composition of the government; conversely, the composition of the government never completely reflects the preferences of the voters at any single point in time.

Consequently, the preferences of individual political actors, and the aggregate preferences of the elected branches of government, will never be perfectly aligned, and often will be in sharp conflict. Every election features important recent events, fresh issues, and new ideas that shift the preferences of voters and alter the electoral choices they make. All Americans are represented in the House, the Senate, and the presidency, but the differing aggregation systems—House districts, states in the Senate, and an indirect national vote for the presidency—create three bodies that, even if wholly elected at the exact same time, would sum to different preferences over policy.

Likewise, the varying length of terms for each of the elected branches creates different incentives and structures the political preferences of the actors. As the framers surmised, the shorter terms of Representatives would likely make them more responsive to rapid shifts in public opinion among their constituents, while the longer terms of Senators would insulate them against being aroused by quickly extinguished passions of public opinion.[73] In addition to these regular time horizons for elections, the presidency now has a fixed time horizon;[74] with a maximum of eight years in office, Presidents have strong incentives to move quickly to achieve their policy goals. Representatives and Senators, without such existential term limits, may often see less need for hurried action.[75]

Vague Powers

The vagueness of much of the Constitution also creates political conflict between the branches. The Constitution, by global standards, is very brief.[76] And while some of the authorities it assigns are uncontestable directives or rules, much of it is open to a variety of interpretations. Not surprisingly, political actors in the different branches are likely to interpret its dictates in ways that enhance or expand their own authority. This is especially true in areas where there are clearly shared responsibilities, such as war powers. The President is commander in chief of the armed forces under Article II,[77] but Congress is granted the authority to declare war, raise and support an army and navy, and make rules governing the armed forces.[78]

Unconsidered Questions

The political branches of the federal government also routinely come into conflict over questions that the Constitution never contemplates. No 18th century document could have foreseen the developments of a nation over centuries, and conflicts between the President and Congress often involve issues that would have never even occurred to the framers as important. Even powers that are seemingly firmly entrenched with one branch or another can generate conflict over their application. For example, only Congress has the power to appropriate funds for an activity of the federal government. But does the President have the discretion to not spend funds appropriated by Congress?[79]

Institutional Power

It is not surprising that the branches of government will seek to enhance their power within the federal government. Since such enhancements of power largely come at the expense of one of the other branches of the government, each branch also has strong incentives to defend its own power from encroachment by the other branches.[80] Such attempts at enhancement and defenses against the encroachments of the other branches can take many forms. Discussed here are three general aspects of the strategies used by the branches.

Asserting and Guarding Power

The most basic institutional strategy for enhancing power is to simply assert it in the course of executing policy preferences, or suggest new powers via legislative proposals. The President may decide that military action is needed and choose not to consult with Congress.[81] The President may decide Senate confirmation of a nominee is taking too long and make a recess appointment while the Senate is in recess for just a few hours.[82] Congress may decide that an investigation of perceived wrongdoing at the White House or in the executive branch is necessary, and subpoena documents and records that may be protected by executive privilege.[83] Congress may design a regulatory agency whose principal officials are not nominated by the President.[84] Left unchallenged by the other branch, these actions will not only take effect, but they will potentially set historical precedent for similar future actions, normalize the action in the mind of the public, or lay the groundwork for further enhancements of power in the same vein.

Therefore, it is common for each branch to strongly guard its power and challenge attempts by the other branches to assert new or enhanced power. Such guarding of power takes many forms. Often, it is simply public repudiation. If one branch asserts a power and another publicly condemns it, public opinion may quickly force the asserting branch to back down. In 1937 President Roosevelt made legislative proposals to expand the Supreme Court and to reorganize the executive branch.[85] Many in Congress saw these bills as attempts to increase executive power over the courts and public policy, and opponents of the measures came to label them "court-packing" and the "dictator bill."[86] Both measures failed, and Roosevelt was widely repudiated for the attempted power grab. Absent mobilized public opinion, the branches also have the ability to guard their power through lawsuit in the federal courts. Conflicts between the executive and legislative branches may result in one party making a legal claim that the other has exceeded its constitutional authority.[87] In other cases, private citizens may bring federal claims against one of the branches asserting an action exceeded the authority of the branch.[88]

Public Prestige

Because public opinion shapes the actions of political actors and thus policy outcomes, the maintenance and enhancement of the power of the branches can be augmented by increasing the public prestige of the institution. If voters believe that one branch of government is more or less capable of dealing with public policy problems or other political issues, power is likely to flow toward that branch of government and away from the other branches. In effect, the institutional reputation of the branches at any given moment affects their relative political power and shapes outcomes, particularly in conflicts that arise between the branches. Many things can affect the public prestige of the branches: perceptions about competence, scandal, attacks from the other branches, etc.[89]

In many respects, the legislative branch has the most difficulty maintaining its public prestige. The President has the advantage of unity of voice, and relatively rarely does the executive branch appear to be in-fighting.[90] In recent times, the Supreme Court has enjoyed strong public opinion support, and enjoys an apolitical reputation that it closely guards.[91] Congress, however, has neither of these advantages. Disagreement is natural in a legislature, and it is rare for Congress to work either quickly or in a completely united fashion.[92] While these features are often beneficial, they work against Congress as a prestigious institution, particularly in situations where the President can project a single solution or plan while simultaneously portraying Congress as deadlocked and chaotic.[93]

Political Capacity

The three branches of the federal government can also work to enhance their political capacity, by seeking to augment the resources available to them for public political confrontations. Effecting outcomes in public policy debates often requires the ability to gather and analyze information, research and develop arguments, and package and reach a public audience with the information. In a public policy fight between two entities, the one with the greater resources that can be mobilized will often have an advantage.[94]

Therefore, the branches of the government can seek to enhance their own power through the enlargement of their own political capacity. This can take the form of greater staffing, such as the expansion of congressional staff under the 1946 Legislative Reorganization Act.[95] Or it can take the form of the creation of entirely new branch-wide entities, such as the creation of the Executive Office of the President or the Congressional Budget Office or the Federal Judicial Center.[96] In many cases, increases in one branch's capacity is acquiesced to by the other branches; Congress routinely passes legislation increasing executive capacity, and the President often consents to increased legislative capacity by refraining from vetoing such legislation.

Consequences for Individual Political Actors

While the three branches of government themselves have strong incentives to maintain and enhance their power, individual political actors within the branches may often find themselves placed at cross-purposes, where the goal of enhancing power for their institution may come into conflict with other political goals they are seeking to achieve.

Cross-Purposes

Generally, three types of goals may create cross-purpose conflicts for political actors seeking to maintain the institutional power of their branch. First, long-term institutional power may come into conflict with personal policy positions. For example, an individual Justice's belief may favor an outcome of a Supreme Court case that may decrease the prestige of the Court; an individual Member of Congress may believe that foreign policy actions taken by the executive branch without the input, or against the majority wishes, of Congress may be the correct decisions; and the President may be unwilling to veto legislation that achieves policy outcomes he prefers despite doing so in a way that reduces executive branch capacity.

A second cross-purpose conflict is one that brings institutional power into conflict with partisan affiliation. Members of a political party generally do not to want to embarrass co-partisans or damage the reputation of their party; instead, they seek to enhance the reputation and brand-name of their party in the hopes of accumulating party power and gaining greater control over public policy.[97] It thus often becomes the case that individuals must choose between helping their political party and enhancing the power of their institution. For example, Representatives may refrain from criticizing the actions of a President from their own party, even when such actions are to the detriment of Congress as an institution. The Representative may judge that the benefit to their constituents, party, or ideological policy preferences outweigh the diminishment of power to the institution.[98]

A third cross-purpose conflict is when electoral goals conflict with institutional power. This can happen when candidates for office believe that attacking or maligning the power of the institution they are seeking to join will be an effective campaign strategy. Candidates for Congress commonly describe Congress as "broken" or "dysfunctional."[99] Nominees for the Supreme Court often warn in Senate hearings about the need to limit the scope or authority of the Court;[100] and candidates for President routinely attack their predecessors for actions that they believe are overreaches of executive power.[101]

A Particularly Congressional Problem

The problem of institutional power coming into conflict with other goals is particularly acute for Congress, especially in relation to the executive branch. As individual members of a large body, Representatives and Senators may not believe they have the responsibility or the capacity to defend the institution.[102] Those who may feel such responsibility, such as party and chamber leaders, will often find themselves in situations in which policy or party goals, either their own personal ones or those of their caucus, come into direct conflict with institutional goals. Even when Congress does choose to institutionally defend itself, it often finds itself speaking with less than a unified voice, as only the most vital institutional powers have the ability to unanimously unify Congress.[103]

These problems of collective action—the responsibility/capacity to defend the institution, the ability to speak with a unified voice, and the conflict with party or policy goals—rarely if ever occur in the executive branch. The unitary nature of the presidency ensures that the executive branch will ultimately always speak with one voice, and past presidents have often expressed— both in office and after retirement—a deep feeling of responsibility for the maintenance of the powers of the presidency.[104] Finally, it is more unusual for party or policy goals to be directly at odds with executive branch power than congressional power, simply because the President in modern times exerts significant control over both his party's politics and the general public policy agenda. His proposals, therefore, tend to set the agenda and, not surprisingly, they are typically very consonant with executive branch power.

Lessons for Those Seeking to Increase Institutional Power

While the cross-purposes that place political actors in conflicted situations with respect to institutional power can seem daunting, they also suggest structural situations in which those seeking to enhance institutional power can harness these cross-purposes and use them for the benefit of the institution. In some cases, the partisan or ideological or electoral goals of political actors align with the institutional goals of the branch. It is in these situations that those seeking greater institutional power, particularly in Congress, can most effectively achieve their goals.

The arrangement of parties, ideologies, and institutions has many variations. Imagine a stylized America with a liberal and conservative political party, whose core principles tended to either favor executive power or legislative power, but varied over time. In this arrangement, with two institutions (Presidency, Congress), two parties (Party A, Party B), and two philosophies about governance (executive-centered, Congress-centered), eight possible arrangements of government are possible. Some of these arrangements are unlikely to be hospitable to the promotion of congressional power. For instance, when one party controls both institutions and has an executive-centered governing philosophy, enhancing congressional power will be quite difficult. On the other hand, when Party A controls the presidency and Party B controls Congress, if Party B has a Congress-centered philosophy for governing, the most hospitable alignment has been achieved.

Those seeking to enhance congressional power will likely achieve their best results in situations of divided government, when the control of Congress is in the hands of a party that naturally is more wary of executive power. In these situations, the partisan, ideological, and institutional incentives all favor an increase of congressional power. There are fewer cross-pressures to conflict members; enhancing congressional power will serve the interests of the institution, the party, and the ideological goals of many members.

Contemporary Issues

Clashes between the branches over the proper division of constitutional power and authority have arisen routinely in recent Congresses, as they have throughout American history. Recent issues include the following:

- War Powers. The 2011 U.S. military operations in Libya raised concerns among some in Congress that the President lacked authority to engage in such operations without congressional approval. What limits can Congress place on Presidential military action?[105]
- Policy implementation. In 2014, the House of Representatives voted to authorize the Speaker to initiate legal action against the executive branch for implementing aspects of the Affordable Care Act in a manner contrary to the statutory language. What implementation latitude does the administration have under law, and can Congress

seek legal enforcement against administration implementation decisions?[106]

- Congressional organization of the judiciary. In 2015, the Supreme Court examined the question of whether Congress could charge non Article-III courts with certain adjudication tasks. What types of courts can Congress create that do not provide Article III protections to their judges? [107]
- Recess Appointments. In 2011, President Obama made several recess appointments while the Senate was in pro-forma session, which led to a lawsuit and ultimately a Supreme Court decision invalidating the appointments. Under what conditions can the President make a recess appointment?[108]
- Recognition of foreign governments. Does Congress have a role in foreign policy that gives it the authority to recognize foreign governments for some purposes, or does the sole power of recognition lie with the President?[109]
- Congressional Oversight and Contempt Power. After the Department of Justice refused to provide subpoenaed documents to the House Oversight and Government Reform Committee, the committee voted to cite the Attorney General for contempt, and the Administration invoked executive privilege as the justification for withholding the documents. To what extent does Congress have a right to executive branch documents? Can Congress force a criminal contempt prosecution to be opened?[110]

CONCLUDING OBSERVATIONS

Two general observations warrant mentioning. First, the contemporary balance of power between the President, Congress, and the courts is not the same as it was in 1789, and is perhaps not the balance intended or expected by the framers of the Constitution. A myriad of changes, developments, and specific events in the United States—ranging from amendments to the Constitution to development in technology to the continuing evolution of American political culture—have continually influenced public opinion, political norms, and the behavior of political actors in ways that have rearranged the relative powers of the institutions.

Second, the relative power of the President, Congress, and the courts is not on any specific trajectory. At various times since the ratification of the Constitution, the power of each institution has been at times ascendant and at other times on the decline. While specific events and developments may predictably lead to an increase or decrease in relative power for one of the branches, predicting the actual future direction of power shifts between the branches is an inherently difficult task. Many events that alter the power balance are either contingent or otherwise rely on the individual actions of political actors.

End Notes

[1] James Madison, "The Federalist No. 47," in Alexander Hamilton, James Madison, and John Jay, The Federalist Papers (Clinton Rossiter, ed.) (New York: Penguin, 1961), p. 301.

[2] Arthur, Gunlicks, Comparing Liberal Democracies (Bloomington, IN: iUniverse, 2011), p. 26. For further discussion of parliamentary systems in comparison with separation of powers systems, see Arend Lijphart, Parliamentary Versus Presidential Government (London: Oxford University Press, 1992); Matthew Soberg Shugart and John M. Carey, Presidents and Assemblies: Constitutional Design and Electoral Dynamics (New York: Cambridge University Press, 1992); Terry M. Moe and Michael Caldwell, "The Institutional Foundations of Democratic Government: A Comparison of Presidential and Parliamentary Systems," Journal of Institutional and Theoretical Economics, vol. 57, no. 2 (1994); Bruce Ackerman, "The New Separation of Powers," Harvard Law Review, vol. 113, no. 3 (2000).

[3] E.E. Schattschnieder, Party Government (New York: Farrar and Rinehart, 1942), p. 1; John Gerring, Strom C. Thacker, and Carola Moreno, "Are Parliamentary Systems Better?" Comparative Political Studies, vol. 42, no. 3 (March 2009), p. 330; Matthew Soberg Shugart, "The Inverse Relationship Between Party Strength and Executive Strength: A Theory of Politicians' Constitutional Choices," British Journal of Political Science, vol. 28, no. 1 (1998).

[4] Gerring, Thacker, and Moreno, "Are Parliamentary Systems Better?" p. 334; Juan Jose Linz, "The Perils of Presidentialism," Journal of Democracy, vol. 1., no. 1 (1990).

[5] Linz, "Perils of Presidentialism," p. 258.

[6] This is not to say that a similar public consensus existed. Indeed, as the ratification process proceeded in 1787 and 1788, organized opposition to the new Constitution arose in most states.

[7] Aristotle, Benjamin Jowett, and H. W. Carless Davis (translators), Aristotle's Politics (Oxford: Clarendon Press, 1920), pp. 84-87; Thomas L. Pangle, Aristotle's Teaching in the "Politics" (Chicago: The University of Chicago Press, 2013), pp. 195-197.

[8] Robert Niven Gilchrist, Principles of Political Science (New York: Longmans, Green, and Co., 1921), p. 289.

[9] These philosophers include Polybius in The Histories, Cicero in The Republic, Aquinas in Summa Theologica, and Machiavelli in Discourses. Polybius,W. R. Paton, F. W.Walbank, and Christian Habicht, The Histories, Volume I-VI (Cambridge: Harvard University Press , 2011); Thomas Aquinas, The Summa Theologica (Westminster, MD: Christian Classics,

1981); Marcus Tullius Cicero, J.G.F. Powell, and J.A. North, Cicero's Republic (London: Institute of Classical Studies, 2001); Nicollo Machiavelli, Ninian Hill Thomspon, Discourses (New York: BN Publishing, 2005).

[10] John Locke and Peter Laslett, Two Treatises of Government (New York: Mentor Books, 1965).

[11] Charles de Secondat, Baron de Montesquieu, and Thomas Nugent, Sprit of Laws (New York: The Colonial Press, 1899), p. 151.

[12] Ibid., p. 160.

[13] Ibid., p. 160.

[14] James Madison, "The Federalist No. 51," in Alexander Hamilton, James Madison, and John Jay, The Federalist Papers (Clinton Rossiter, ed.) (New York: Penguin, 1961), p. 322.

[15] Spirit of Laws, pp. 151-159.

[16] James Madison, "The Federalist No. 47," in Alexander Hamilton, James Madison, and John Jay, The Federalist Papers (Clinton Rossiter, ed.) (New York: Penguin, 1961), p. 301.

[17] Ibid., p. 311.

[18] Richard C. Simmons, The American Colonies: From Settlement to Independence (London: Longman, 1976), pp. 245- 258. See also Alison G. Olson, "Eighteenth Century Colonial Legislatures and Their Constituents," The Journal of American History, vol. 79, no. 2 (September 1992); Jack P. Greene, "The Role of the Lower Houses of Assembly in Eighteenth Century Politics," Journal of Southern History, vol. 27, no. 4 (November 1961).

[19] John A. Fairlie, "The Veto Power of the State Governor," The American Political Science Review, vol. 11, no. 3 (August 1917), pp. 473-474.

[20] Simmons, The American Colonies, p. 256.

[21] Bernard, Bailyn, The Origins of American Politics (New York: Vintage, 1968); Wesley Frank Craven, The Colonies in Transition, 1660-1713 (New York: Harper and Row: 1968).

[22] Charles McLean Andrews, The Colonial Background of the American Revolution (New Haven: Yale University Press, 1924).

[23] Ibid.

[24] Ibid.

[25] Ibid.

[26] Gordon Wood, The Creation of the American Republic, 1776-1787 (New York: Norton and Co.: 1969), pp. 127-160.

[27] Willi Adams, The First American Constitutions: Republican Ideology and the meaning of the State Constitutions (Lanham, MD: Rowman and Littlefield: 2001); Lawrence M. Friedman, "State Constitutions in Historical Perspective," Annals of the American Academy of Political and Social Science, vol. 496, no. 1 (March 1988), pp. 33-42.

[28] Virginia Constitution (1776), § 6; Delaware Constitution (1776) § 7; New Jersey Constitution (1776) § 7.

[29] Pennsylvania Constitution (1776) § 3.

[30] Articles of Confederation (1781) § IX.

[31] New Yok Constitution (1776) § XVII.

[32] Massachusetts Constitution (1780) § XXX.

[33] Wood, The Creation of the American Republic, p. 161.

[34] Ibid., pp. 393-467.

[35] Jack Rakove, "The Legacy of the Articles of Confederation," Publius, vol. 12, no. 4 (Autumn 1982), pp. 45-66.

[36] James Madison, "The Federalist No. 10," in Alexander Hamilton, James Madison, and John Jay, The Federalist Papers (Clinton Rossiter, ed.) (New York: Penguin, 1961), pp. 77-83.

[37] James Madison, "The Federalist No. 47," in Alexander Hamilton, James Madison, and John Jay, The Federalist Papers (Clinton Rossiter, ed.) (New York: Penguin, 1961), p. 301.

[38] In addition, the Framers also set up a federal system in which the states maintained certain sovereign functions and the central government had limited powers. A full discussion of federalism, however, is beyond the scope of this report. For a general discussion of federalism, see CRS Report RL30315, Federalism, State Sovereignty, and the Constitution: Basis and Limits of Congressional Power, by Kenneth R. Thomas.

[39] United States Constitution, Article I §1

[40] United States Constitution, Article II §1

[41] United States Constitution, Article III §1

[42] United States Constitution, Article I §6, clause 2.

[43] Ibid.

[44] United States Constitution, Article II §1, clause 2.

[45] Ibid. Under the Constitution, Congress does have a role in the election of the President and Vice President if no candidate receives a majority of the electoral votes. See United States Constitution, Article II §1, clause 3.

[46] United States Constitution, Article I §2, clause 1; Amendment XVII, clause 1.

[47] United States Constitution, Article III §1.

[48] For an overview of the legislative branch and its organizations, see CRS Report R44029, Legislative Branch: FY2016 Appropriations, by Ida A. Brudnick.

[49] For an overview of the President's available resources in the Executive Office of the President, see CRS Report 98- 606, The Executive Office of the President: An Historical Overview, by Barbara L. Schwemle, available upon request.

[50] For an overview of the judiciary's resources, see CRS Report R44078, Judiciary Appropriations FY2016, by Matthew E. Glassman.

[51] United States Constitution, Article II §1, clause 7.

[52] United States Constitution, Article III §1.

[53] Richard Neustadt, Presidential Power and the Modern Presidents (New York: The Free Press: 1990), p. x.

[54] United States Constitution, Article I §7, clause 2; Article II § 2, clause 2.

[55] United States Constitution, Article III §2.

[56] United States Constitution, Article I §9, clause 7.

[57] United States Constitution, Article III §1.

[58] United States Constitution, Article II §2, clause 2.

[59] United States Constitution, Amendment 25, §2.

[60] United States Constitution, Article II §4; Article I § 2, clause 5; §3, clause 6.

[61] The Speech or Debate Clause places significant limitations on the ability of the executive branch to both investigate and prosecute Members of Congress for violations of the law. For an overview of the Speech or Debate Clause see CRS Report R42648, The Speech or Debate Clause: Constitutional Background and Recent Developments, by Alissa M. Dolan and Todd Garvey.

[62] Representatives have very limited immunity from certain laws. See CRS Legal Sidebar WSLG154, Are Members of Congress Above the Law?, by Jack Maskell.

[63] For a brief overview, see CRS In Focus IF10015, Congressional Oversight and Investigations, by Alissa M. Dolan, Todd Garvey, and Walter J. Oleszek.

[64] United States Constitution, Article II §2.

[65] United States Constitution, Article I §8.

[66] United States Constitution, Article I §9, clause 7.

[67] United States Constitution, Article II §3, Article II §2, clause 2.

[68] Charles Stewart III, "Congress and the Constitutional System," In Paul J. Quirk and Sarah A. Binder, Institutions of American Democracy: The Legislative Branch (New York: Oxford University Press, 2005), p. 23. For further information on congressional-executive agreements and treaties, see CRS Report 97-896, Why Certain Trade Agreements Are Approved as Congressional-Executive Agreements Rather Than Treaties, by Jane M. Smith, Daniel T. Shedd, and Brandon J. Murrill.

[69] This stands in sharp contrast to the traditional parliamentary model of republican government, which generally produces unified governments. See Gerring, Thacker, and Moreno, "Are Parliamentary Systems Better?" p. 334; Juan Jose Linz, "The Perils of Presidentialism," Journal of Democracy, vol. 1., no. 1 (1990).

[70] United States Constitution, Article I §2. See also CRS Report R42831, Congressional Redistricting: An Overview, by Royce Crocker.

[71] United States Constitution, Article I §3; Amendment XVII.

[72] United States Constitution, Article II §1; Amendment XII.

[73] James Madison, "The Federalist No. 62," in Alexander Hamilton, James Madison, and John Jay, The Federalist Papers (Clinton Rossiter, ed.) (New York: Penguin, 1961), pp. 376-390.

[74] United States Constitution, Amendment XXII.

[75] Douglas L. Kriner and Andrew Reeves, The Particularistic President: Executive Branch Politics and Political Inequality (New York: Cambridge University Press, 2015), pp. 16; William G. Howell, Thinking About the Presidency: The Primacy of Power (Princeton: Princeton University Press, 2013).

[76] The U.S. Constitution is less than 4400 words, making it one of the shortest Constitutions. See Christopher W. Hammons, "Was James Madison Wrong? Rethinking the American Preference for Short, Framework-Oriented Constitutions," The American Political Science Review, Vol. 93, No. 4 (December, 1999), pp. 837-849.

[77] United States Constitution, Article II §2.

[78] United States Constitution, Article I §8.

[79] Train v. City of New York, 420 U.S. 35 (1975).

[80] David Mayhew, The Electoral Connection (New Haven: Yale University Press, 1973); Richard Fenno, Homestyle: House Members in Their Districts (New York: Pearson, 2002).

[81] Louis Fisher, Presidential War Power (Lawrence, KS: University of Kansas Press, 1995).

[82] See CRS Report R42323, President Obama's January 4, 2012, Recess Appointments: Legal Issues, by David H. Carpenter et al.

[83] CRS Legal Sidebar WSLG86, Presidential Claims of Executive Privilege, by Todd Garvey.

[84] Buckley v. Valeo, 424 U.S. 1 (1976).

[85] Burt Solomon, FDR v. The Constitution: The Court-Packing Fight and the Triumph of Democracy (New York: Walker, 2009); Stephen Skowronek, The Politics Presidents Make (Cambridge, MA: Belknap Press, 1993).

[86] Gregory A. Caldeira, "Public Opinion and the U.S. Supreme Court: FDR's Court-Packing Plan," The American Political Science Review, vol. 81, no. 4 (December 1987), pp. 1139-1153; Barry D. Karl, "Executive Reorganization and Presidential Power," The Supreme Court Review, vol. 1977 (1977), pp. 1-37.

[87] See CRS Legal Sidebar WSLG172, House Committee Files Suit to Compel Production of Fast and Furious Documents, by Todd Garvey.

[88] CRS Legal Sidebar WSLG566, Supreme Court to Hear Appointments Case, by David H. Carpenter.

[89] For example, see James Sundquist, The Decline and Resurgence of Congress (Washington: The Brookings Institution, 1981).

[90] Charles Hardin, "The Crisis and Its Cure," in William Lasser, Perspectives on American Politics (Boston; Wadsworth, 2012), p. 299.

[91] See http://www.gallup.com/poll/4732/supreme-court.aspx.

[92] Fenno, Homestyle, p. 194.

[93] Michael Foley and John E. Owens, Congress and the Presidency: Institutional Politics in a Separated System (Manchester, UK: Manchester University Press, 1996), pp. 405-407.

[94] For example, see Matthew Glassman, "Congressional Leadership: A Resource Perspective," in Jacob Straus, Party and Procedure in the United States Congress (New York: Rowan and Littlefield, 2011).

[95] 60 Stat. 812, August 2, 1946.

[96] 53 Stat. 561, April 3, 1939; 88 Stat. 297, July 12, 1974; 81 Stat. 664, December 20, 1967.

[97] David Mayhew, Divided We Govern (New Haven: Yale University Press, 1991), p. 3; Morris S. Ogul, Congress Overseas the Bureaucracy (Pittsburgh: University of Pittsburg Press, 1976), p. 18.

[98] Charles Stewart III, "Congress and the Constitutional System," In Paul J. Quirk and Sarah A. Binder, Institutions of American Democracy: The Legislative Branch (New York: Oxford University Press, 2005), p. 23.

[99] Fenno, Homestyle, p. 197.

[100] For example, see "Transcript: Day One of the Roberts Hearings," The Washington Post, September 13, 2005, http://www.washingtonpost.com/wp-dyn/content/article/2005/09/13/AR2005091300693.html.

[101] For example, then-Senator Obama routinely criticized then-President George W. Bush for expanding executive power, resulting in short video clips from the 2008 campaign (such as https://www.youtube.com/watch?v= a3IWq3CXHyc) that were later used as political attacks against him as President.

[102] Mayhew, The Electoral Connection.

[103] Stewart, "Congress and the Constitutional System," p. 23.

[104] For example, see the discussion of President Nixon's desire to protect the presidency in Mark J. Rozell, Executive Privilege: The Dilemma of Secrecy and Democratic Accountability (Baltimore: John Hopkins University Press, 1994), pp. 77-79.

[105] For background on Member use of litigation in regard to war powers disputes, see CRS Report R41989, Congressional Authority to Limit Military Operations, by Jennifer K. Elsea, Michael John Garcia, and Thomas J. Nicola; CRS Report RL30352, War Powers Litigation Initiated by Members of Congress Since the Enactment of the War Powers Resolution, by Michael John Garcia.

[106] H.Res. 676, 113th Congress. For background on the Affordable Care Act provisions in question, see CRS Legal Sidebar WSLG582, Obama Administration Delays Implementation of ACA's Employer Responsibility Requirements: A Brief Legal Overview, by Jennifer A. Staman, Daniel T. Shedd, and Edward C. Liu.

[107] For more information, see CRS Legal Sidebar WSLG1274, Function Over Form: The Role of Consent and the Supreme Court's Latest Separation of Powers Decision in Wellness Int'l v. Sharif, by Andrew Nolan.

[108] See CRS Report R42323, President Obama's January 4, 2012, Recess Appointments: Legal Issues, by David H. Carpenter et al.; CRS Report R43030, The Recess Appointment Power After Noel Canning v. NLRB: Constitutional Implications, by Todd Garvey and David H. Carpenter.

[109] CRS Report R43773, Zivotofsky v. Kerry: The Jerusalem Passport Case and Its Potential Implications for Congress's Foreign Affairs Powers, by Jennifer K. Elsea; CRS Legal Sidebar WSLG1287, Has Congress Lost its Voice on Jerusalem? (Zivotofsky Part I), by Jennifer K. Elsea; CRS Legal Sidebar WSLG1288, Youngstown Revisited (Zivotofsky Part II), by Jennifer K. Elsea.

[110] See CRS Legal Sidebar WSLG81, A Holder Contempt Citation: Legally Enforceable?, by Todd Garvey; CRS Report R42670, Presidential Claims of Executive Privilege: History, Law, Practice, and Recent Developments, by Todd Garvey and Alissa M. Dolan; CRS Recorded Event WRE00052, The Holder Contempt: A Case Study in Congress's Authority to Enforce Subpoenas, by Todd Garvey and Alissa M. Dolan.

In: Separation of Powers …
Editor: Josephine Spencer
ISBN: 978-1-63485-189-3

Chapter 2

FEDERALISM, STATE SOVEREIGNTY, AND THE CONSTITUTION: BASIS AND LIMITS OF CONGRESSIONAL POWER*

Kenneth R. Thomas

SUMMARY

The lines of authority between states and the federal government are, to a significant extent, defined by the United States Constitution and relevant case law. In recent years, however, the Supreme Court has decided a number of cases that would seem to reevaluate this historical relationship. This report discusses state and federal legislative power generally, focusing on a number of these "federalism" cases. The report does not, however, address the larger policy issue of when it is appropriate—as opposed to constitutionally permissible—to exercise federal powers.

The U.S. Constitution provides that Congress shall have the power to regulate commerce with foreign nations and among the various states. This power has been cited as the constitutional basis for a significant portion of the laws passed by Congress over the last 50 years, and, in conjunction with the Necessary and Proper Clause, it currently represents one of the broadest bases for the exercise of congressional powers. In

* This is an edited, reformatted and augmented version of a Congressional Research Service publication RL30315, prepared for Members and Committees of Congress, dated September 23, 2013.

United States v. Lopez and subsequent cases, however, the Supreme Court did bring into question the extent to which Congress can rely on the Commerce Clause as a basis for federal jurisdiction.

Another significant source of congressional power is the Fourteenth Amendment, specifically the Equal Protection and Due Process Clauses. Section 5 of that amendment provides that Congress has the power to enforce its provisions. In the case of *Flores v. City of Boerne*, however, the Court imposed limits on this power, requiring that there must be a "congruence and proportionality" between the injury to be remedied and the law adopted to that end.

The Tenth Amendment provides that "powers not delegated to the United States by the Constitution, nor prohibited by it to the States, are reserved to the States respectively, or to the people." While this language would appear to represent one of the most clear examples of a federalist principle in the Constitution, it has not had a significant impact in limiting federal powers. However, in *New York v. United States* and *Printz v. United States*, the Court did find that, under the Tenth Amendment, Congress cannot "commandeer" either the legislative process of a state or the services of state executive branch officials.

The Eleventh Amendment provides that "[t]he Judicial power of the United States shall not be construed to extend to any suit in law or equity, commenced or prosecuted against one of the United States by Citizens of another State." Although this text is limited to preventing citizens from bringing diversity cases against states in federal courts, the Supreme Court has expanded the concept of state sovereign immunity further to prohibit citizens generally from bringing suits against states under federal law generally. There are exceptions to this limitation, however, and Congress also has a limited ability to abrogate such state immunity.

Finally, Congress has the power under the Spending Clause to require states to undertake certain activities as a condition of receiving federal monies. Such conditions, however, must be related to the underlying grant, and the financial consequences of non-compliance cannot be coercive. Further, if the condition relates to the creation of a "new and independent" program, and if the amount to be withheld represents a significant portion of a state's overall budget, then such condition will be found to violate federalism principles.

The lines of authority between states and the federal government are, to a significant extent, defined by the United States Constitution and relevant case law. In recent years, however, the Supreme Court has decided a number of cases that would seem to be a reevaluation of this historical relationship. This report discusses state and federal legislative power generally and focuses on a number of these "federalism" cases. The report discusses state and federal legislative power generally, and focuses on a number of these "federalism" cases.[1] Issues addressed include congressional power under the Commerce Clause and the Fourteenth Amendment; limits on congressional powers, such as the Tenth Amendment; state sovereign immunity under the Eleventh Amendment; and grant condition imposed under the Spending Clause. The report does not, however, address the much larger federalism issue of when it is appropriate—as opposed to constitutionally permissible—for federal powers to be exercised.

POWERS OF THE STATES

States may generally legislate on all matters within their territorial jurisdiction. This "police power" does not arise from the Constitution, but is an inherent attribute of the states' territorial sovereignty. The Constitution does, however, provide certain specific limitations on that power. For instance, a state is relatively limited in its authority regarding the regulation of foreign imports and exports[2] or the conduct of foreign affairs.[3] Further, states must respect the decisions of courts of other states,[4] and are limited in their ability to vary their territory without congressional permission.[5] In addition, the Supreme Court has found that states are limited in their ability to burden interstate commerce.[6]

POWERS OF THE FEDERAL GOVERNMENT

The powers of the federal government, while limited to those enumerated in the Constitution,[7] have been interpreted broadly, so as to create a large potential overlap with state authority. For instance, Article I, Section 8, cl. 18 provides that "[t]he Congress shall have power ... To make all laws which shall be necessary and proper for carrying into Execution the foregoing Powers, and all other Powers vested by this Constitution in the Government of the United States, or in any Department or Officer thereof." Early in the history of the Constitution, the Supreme Court found that this clause enlarges rather than narrows the powers of Congress.[8]

Congress has broad financial powers, including the power to tax and spend in order to pay debts and provide for the common defense and general welfare of the United States.[9] Congress also has the power to borrow money and to appropriate money from the United States Treasury.[10] The purposes for which Congress may tax and spend are very broad and are not limited by the scope of other enumerated powers under which Congress may regulate.[11] On the other hand, Congress has no power to regulate "for the general welfare," but may only tax and spend for that purpose.

Congress also has broad authority over the commercial interests of the nation, including the power to regulate commerce,[12] to establish bankruptcy laws,[13] to coin money,[14] to punish counterfeiters,[15] to establish post offices and post roads,[16] and to grant patents and copyrights.[17] The Commerce Clause, discussed in more detail below, is one of the most far-reaching grants of power to Congress. Regulation of interstate commerce covers all movement of people and things across state lines, including communication and transportation.

Congress has broad powers over citizenship, including the power to define the circumstances under which immigrants may become citizens,[18] and to protect the rights of those persons who have citizenship. The Fourteenth Amendment gives Congress the power to enforce the guarantees of the Fourteenth Amendment, including the right to due process and equal protection.[19] This power extends specifically to the power of Congress to protect the rights of citizens who are at least 18[20] to vote regardless of race, color, previous condition of servitude,[21] or sex.[22] Congress may also regulate the time, place, and manner of federal elections,[23] and judge the result of such elections.[24] Congress also has a number of other powers relating to elections and appointments.[25]

Congress has the power and authority to purchase and administer property, and has power over those jurisdictions that are not controlled by states, such as the District of Columbia and the territories.[26] Congress is limited by the Fifth Amendment, however, in the taking of private property without compensation.[27] Congress has numerous powers related to war and the protection of the United States and its sovereign interests.[28]

THE COMMERCE CLAUSE

As noted above, the U.S. Constitution provides that Congress shall have the power to regulate commerce with foreign nations and among the various states.[29] This power has been cited as the constitutional basis for a significant portion of the laws passed by Congress over the last 50 years, and it currently represents one of the broadest bases for the exercise of congressional powers. In *United States v. Lopez*,[30] however, the Supreme Court brought into question the extent to which Congress can rely on the Commerce Clause as a basis for federal jurisdiction.

Under the Gun-Free School Zones Act of 1990, Congress made it a federal offense for "any individual knowingly to possess a firearm at a place that the individual knows, or has reasonable cause to believe, is a school zone."[31] In *Lopez*, the Court held that, because the act neither regulated a commercial activity nor contained a requirement that the possession was connected to interstate commerce, the act exceeded the authority of Congress under the Commerce Clause. Although the Court did not explicitly overrule any previous rulings upholding federal statutes passed under the authority of the Commerce Clause, the decision would appear to suggest new limits to Congress's legislative authority.

The scope and extent of the Commerce Clause does not appear to have been of particular concern to the framers of the Constitution.[32] There are indications that the founding fathers considered the federal regulation of commerce to be an important power of the new Constitution primarily as a means of facilitating trade and of raising revenue.[33] While the Anti-Federalists argued that the new Constitution gave too much power to the federal government, they apparently did not raise significant objections to the granting of power to regulate interstate commerce.[34]

The Supreme Court, however, developed an expansive view of the Commerce Clause relatively early in the history of judicial review. For instance, Chief Justice Marshall wrote in 1824 that "the power over commerce ... is vested in Congress as absolutely as it would be in a single government ..." and that "the influence which their constituents possess at elections, are ... the sole restraints" on this power.[35] However, the issue in most of the early Supreme Court Commerce Clause cases dealt not with the limits of congressional authority, but on the implied limitation of the Commerce Clause on a state's ability to regulate commerce.[36]

It has been suggested that the Commerce Clause should be restricted to the regulation of "selling, buying, bartering and transporting."[37] In fact, much of the federal legislation approved of by the Supreme Court early in the 20th century did relate to issues such as the regulation of lottery tickets,[38] the transporting of adulterated food,[39] and the interstate transportation of prostitutes.[40] Moreover, during the early 1900s, the Supreme Court struck down a series of federal statutes that attempted to extend commerce regulation to activities such as "production," "manufacturing,"[41] and "mining."[42]

Starting in 1937, however, with the decision in *NLRB v. Jones & Laughlin Steel Corporation*,[43] the Supreme Court held that Congress has the ability to protect interstate commerce from burdens and obstructions that "affect" commerce transactions. In the *NLRB* case, the court upheld the National Labor Relations Act, finding that by controlling industrial labor strife, Congress was preventing burdens from being placed on interstate commerce.[44] Thus, the Court rejected previous distinctions between the economic activities (such as manufacturing) that led up to interstate economic transactions, and the interstate transactions themselves. By allowing Congress to regulate activities that were in the "stream" of commerce, the Court also set the stage for the regulation of a variety of other activities that "affect" commerce.

Subsequent Court decisions found that Congress had considerable discretion in determining which activities "affect" interstate commerce, as long as the legislation was "reasonably" related to achieving its goals of regulating interstate commerce.[45] Thus the Court found that in some cases, events of purely local commerce (such as local working conditions) might, because of market forces, negatively affect the regulation of interstate commerce, and thus would be susceptible to regulation.[46] The Court has also held that an activity which in itself does not affect interstate commerce could be regulated if all such activities taken in the aggregate did affect interstate commerce.[47] Under the reasoning of these cases, the Court has upheld many diverse laws, including laws regulating production of wheat on farms,[48] racial discrimination by businesses,[49] and loan-sharking.[50]

The *Lopez* case was significant in that it is the first time since 1937 that the Supreme Court struck down a federal statute purely based on a finding that Congress had exceeded its powers under the Commerce Clause.[51] In doing so, the Court revisited its prior cases, sorted the commerce power into three categories, and asserted that Congress could not go beyond these three categories: (1) regulation of channels of commerce, (2) regulation of instrumentalities of commerce, and (3) regulation of economic activities that "affect" commerce.[52]

Within the third category of activities that "affect commerce," the Court determined that the power to regulate commerce applies to intrastate activities only when they "substantially" affect commerce.[53] Still, the Court in *Lopez* spoke approvingly of earlier cases upholding laws that regulated intrastate credit transactions, restaurants utilizing interstate supplies, and hotels catering to interstate guests. The Court also recognized that while some intrastate activities may by themselves have a trivial effect on commerce, regulation of these activities may be constitutional if their regulation is an essential part of a larger economic regulatory scheme. Thus, the Court even approved what has been perceived as one of its most expansive rulings, *Wickard v. Filburn*, which allowed the regulation of the production and consumption of wheat for home consumption.[54]

The Court in *Lopez* found, however, that the Gun-Free School Zones Act fell into none of the three categories set out above. It held that it is not a regulation of channels of commerce, nor does it protect an instrumentality of commerce. Finally, its effect on interstate commerce was found to be too removed to be "substantial." The Court noted that the regulated activity, possessing guns in school, neither by itself nor in the aggregate affected commercial transactions.[55] Further, the statute contained no requirement that interstate commerce be affected, such as that the gun had been previously transported in interstate commerce.[56] Nor was the criminalization of possession of a gun near a school part of a larger regulatory scheme that did regulate commerce.[57] Finally, the Court indicated that criminal law enforcement is an area of law traditionally reserved to the states.[58] Consequently, the Court found that Congress did not have the authority to pass the Gun-Free School Zone Act.

It should be noted that the *Lopez* Court purported to be limiting, but not overruling, prior case law that had supported an expansive interpretation of the commerce clause. Consequently, most existing federal laws, which have traditionally been drafted to be consistent with this case law,[59] would survive constitutional scrutiny even under *Lopez.* However, in at least one significant case, Congress passed a law, the Violence Against Women Act, that seemed to invoke the same concerns that the Court found in *Lopez*. Consequently, the relevant portion of that act was struck down in *United States v. Morrison.*[60]

In *Morrison*, the Court evaluated whether 42 U.S.C. Section 13981, which provides a federal private right of action for victims of gender-motivated violence, was within the power of Congress to enact under the Commerce Clause. In *Morrison*, the victim of an alleged rape brought suit against the alleged rapist, arguing that this portion of the act was sustainable because it addressed activities that substantially affect interstate commerce.[61] The Court, however, noted that unlike traditional statutes based on the commerce clause, the activity in question had nothing to do with commerce or an economic enterprise. This point had been made previously in *Lopez*, and here the Court reaffirmed the holding that in order to fall under the acceptable category of laws that "substantially affect commerce," the underlying activity itself must generally be economic or commercial.[62] As gender-motivated violence does not inherently relate to an economic activity, the Court held that it was beyond the authority of Congress to regulate.

In the case of *Gonzales v. Raich*,[63] the Court evaluated an "as applied" challenge to the Controlled Substances Act as regards obtaining, manufacturing, or possessing marijuana for medical purposes. The case was brought by two seriously ill residents of California who used marijuana in compliance with the California Compassionate Use Act of 1996.[64] The challenge was based on the argument that the narrow class of activity being engaged in—the intrastate, noncommercial cultivation and possession of cannabis for personal medical purposes as recommended by a patient's physician pursuant to valid California state law—did not have a substantial impact on commerce, and thus could not be regulated under the Commerce Clause.[65]

In upholding the application of the Controlled Substances Act in the *Raich* case, the Court relied on its decision in *Wickard v. Filburn*,[66] which held that "even if appellee's activity be local and though it may not be regarded as commerce, it may still, whatever its nature, be reached by Congress if it exerts a substantial economic effect on interstate commerce."[67] The *Wickard* case upheld the application of the Agricultural Adjustment Act of 1938,[68] which was designed to control prices by regulating the volume of wheat moving in interstate commerce. The Court in *Wickard* held that Congress could regulate not only the wheat sold into commerce, but also wheat retained for consumption on a farm.[69] The Court did so on the theory that the while the impact of wheat consumed on the farm on interstate commerce might be trivial, it was significant when combined with wheat from other farmers similarly situated.[70]

Based on *Wickard*, the Court in *Raich* held that Congress could consider the aggregate effect that allowing the production and consumption of marijuana for medical purposes would have on the illegal market for marijuana.[71] Of even greater concern was that diversion of marijuana grown for medicinal purposes for other uses would frustrate the federal interest in eliminating commercial transactions in the interstate market.[72] In both cases, the Court found that the regulation was within Congress's commerce power because Congress had a rational basis to determine that production of a commodity meant for home consumption, be it wheat or marijuana, could have a substantial effect on supply and demand. In addition, because exempting the use of medical marijuana could undercut enforcement of the Controlled Substances Act, the Court found that the application in this case was within Congress's authority to "make all Laws which shall be necessary and proper" to effectuate its powers.

THE NECESSARY AND PROPER CLAUSE

The Constitution provides Congress not only enumerated powers, but also the ability to pass laws to make such powers effective. While such a power might have been implied of necessity even without an explicit textual basis in the Constitution, the Founding Fathers specifically included congressional authority to "make all Laws which shall be necessary and proper"[73] to effectuate its powers. Although the extension of congressional power under this clause is not an independent basis for legislation, the provision has been integral to a broad interpretation of other congressional powers. For instance, as discussed below, the expansive nature of modern Commerce Clause doctrine may actually be a reflection of Necessary and Proper Clause jurisprudence.

Sometimes, the Court's reliance on the Necessary and Proper Clause in a particular case is only briefly noted, or may even exist *sub silentio*. For instance, the majority opinion in the case of *Gonzales v. Raich* (discussed above) emphasized that, in evaluating the scope of Congress's authority under the Commerce Clause to regulate medicinal marijuana, the Court need only find that Congress had a "rational basis" to find a link between the legislation and the Commerce Clause. The Court then went on to note that in such cases "Congress was acting well within its authority to 'make all Laws which shall be necessary and proper' to 'regulate Commerce ... among the several States.'"[74] This language then served to allow the Court to approve the restriction of medical marijuana as one component of a larger economic regulatory scheme.

This passing reference to the Necessary and Proper Clause may obscure its historical significance to Commerce Clause litigation. Writing in concurrence in *Raich*, Justice Scalia argued that it is more accurate to characterize the expansive "substantial effects" prong of Commerce Clause analysis as predominantly based on the Necessary and Proper Clause. He noted that the current description of the "substantial effects" prong is misleading because, unlike the channels, instrumentalities, and agents of interstate commerce, activities that substantially affect interstate commerce are not themselves part of interstate commerce, and thus the power to regulate them cannot come from the Commerce Clause alone. Rather, "as this Court has acknowledged ...

Congress's regulatory authority over intrastate activities that are not themselves part of interstate commerce (including activities that have a substantial effect on interstate commerce) derives from the Necessary and Proper Clause."[75] In fact, Justice Scalia argues that, in some cases, the Necessary and Proper Clause can go beyond existing doctrines of the

Commerce Clause, to regulate even those intrastate activities that do not themselves substantially affect interstate commerce.

Another area where the Court has provided a similarly broad interpretation of an Article I congressional power based on the Necessary and Proper Clause is the Spending Clause.[76] In *Sabri v. United States*,[77] the Court considered whether the federal government could punish the bribery of state, local, and tribal officials if the governmental entities that employed them received at least $10,000 in federal funds. The defendant, who was convicted of attempting to bribe a city councilman to facilitate the building of a hotel and retail structure in Minneapolis, argued that the statute in question had no federal nexus. The Court rejected this argument, holding that Congress's authority under the Spending Clause, when supplemented by the Necessary and Proper Clause, allowed Congress to ensure that federal dollars not be diverted or undermined by corruption. The Court held that it was not important if the federal funds received by the governmental entity in question were not directly involved in a particular scheme, because "money is fungible, bribed officials are untrustworthy stewards of federal funds, and corrupt contractors do not deliver dollar-for-dollar value."[78]

An even more expansive interpretation of the Necessary and Proper Clause, in this case as applied to the entire federal criminal penal system (which derives from a variety of congressional powers), is found in the Court's opinion in *United States v. Comstock*.[79] In *Comstock*, the Court evaluated a federal statute which allowed for the civil commitment of a federal prisoner past the term of his or her imprisonment, if that prisoner would have serious difficultly in refraining from sexually violent conduct or child molestation. The statute contained no requirement that the threatened future conduct would fall under federal jurisdiction, raising the question of what constitutional basis could be cited for the enforcement of the statute.

The majority opinion in *Comstock* upheld the statute after considering five factors: (1) the historic breadth of the Necessary and Proper Clause; (2) the history of federal involvement in this area; (3) the reason for the statute's enactment; (4) the statute's accommodation of state interests; and (5) whether the scope of the statute was too attenuated from Article I powers.[80] The Court noted that the breadth of the power was established by Justice Marshall in the case of *McCulloch v. Maryland*,[81] where the Chief Justice wrote: "Let the end be legitimate, let it be within the scope of the Constitution, and all means which are appropriate, which are plainly adapted to that end, which are not prohibited, but consist with the letter and spirit of the Constitution, are Constitutional."

Previous federal involvement in the area included not only the civil commitment of defendants who were incompetent to stand trial or who became insane during the course of their imprisonment, but, starting in 1949, the continued confinement of those adjudged incompetent or insane past the end of their prison term.

In upholding the sex offender statute, the Court found that protection of the public and the probability that such prisoners would not be committed by the state represented a rational basis for the passage of such legislation. The Court further found that the state interests were protected by the legislation, as the statute provided for transfer of the committed individuals to state authorities willing to accept them. Finally, the Court found that the statute was not too attenuated from the Article I powers underlying the criminal laws which had been the basis for incarceration, as it related to the responsible administration of the United States prison system.

THE FOURTEENTH AMENDMENT

Another significant source of congressional power is Section 5 of the Fourteenth Amendment. The Fourteenth Amendment provides that states shall not deprive citizens of "life, liberty or property" without due process of law nor deprive them of equal protection of the laws. Section 5 provides that Congress has the power to legislate to enforce the amendment.

The Fourteenth Amendment represented a significant shift of power in the nation's federal system. Until the passage of the Fourteenth Amendment, the Constitution was limited to establishing the powers and limitations of the federal government. However, the amendments passed immediately after the Civil War (the Thirteenth,[82] Fourteenth, and Fifteenth[83] Amendments), dramatically altered this regime. Passage of these amendments subjected a state's control over its own citizens to oversight by either the federal judiciary or Congress. The most significant impact of the Fourteenth Amendment has been its implementation by the federal courts, as state legislation came under scrutiny for having violated due process or equal protection. However, Congress has also seen fit to exercise its power under the Fourteenth Amendment to address issues such as voting rights and police brutality.

The scope of Congress's power under Section 5 of the Fourteenth Amendment, however, has been in flux over the years. In *Katzenbach v. Morgan*,[84] the Court held that Section 5 of the Fourteenth Amendment authorized Congress not just to enforce the provisions of the Fourteenth

Amendment as defined by the courts, but to help define its scope. In *Katzenbach*, the Court upheld a portion of the Voting Rights Act of 1965 that barred the application of English literacy requirements to persons who had reached 6th grade in a Puerto Rican school taught in Spanish. In upholding the statute, the Court rejected the argument that Congress's power to legislate under the Fourteenth Amendment was limited to enforcing that which the Supreme Court found to be a violation of that amendment. Rather, the Court held that Congress could enforce the Fourteenth Amendment by "appropriate" legislation consistent with the "letter and spirit of the constitution."

The rationale for this holding appears to be that Congress has the ability to evaluate and address factual situations that it determines may lead to degradation of rights protected under the Fourteenth Amendment. This is true even if a court would not find a constitutional violation to have occurred. In fact, what the Court appeared to have done was to require only that Congress establish a rational basis for why the legislation was necessary to protect a Fourteenth Amendment right.

Subsequent Supreme Court cases, however, have limited the reach of *Katzenbach.* In *Oregon v. Mitchell,*[85] the Court struck down a requirement that the voting age be lowered to 18 for state elections. In prohibiting Congress from dictating the voting age for state elections, a splintered Court appears to have supported Congress's power to pass laws that protect Fourteenth Amendment rights against state intrusions, but rejected the ability of Congress to extend the substantive content of those rights. As 18-year-olds are not a protected class under the Fourteenth Amendment, the Court found that Congress was attempting to create, rather than protect, Fourteenth Amendment rights.

More recently, in the case of *Flores v. City of Boerne,*[86] the Court struck down the Religious Freedom Restoration Act (RFRA) as beyond the authority of Congress under Section 5 of the Fourteenth Amendment. For many years prior to the passage of RFRA, a law of general applicability restricting the free exercise of religion, to be consistent with the Freedom of Exercise Clause of the First Amendment, had to be justified by a compelling governmental interest. However, in the 1990 case of *Oregon v. Smith,*[87] the Court had lowered this standard. The *Smith* case involved members of the Native American Church who were denied unemployment benefits when they lost their jobs for having used peyote during a religious ceremony. The *Smith* case held that neutral generally applicable laws may be applied to religious practices even if the law is not supported by a compelling governmental interest. RFRA, in response, was an attempt by Congress to overturn the *Smith* case, and to require a compelling governmental interest when a state applied a generally applied law to religion.

The *City of Boerne* case arose when the City of Boerne denied a church a building permit to expand, because the church was in a designated historical district. The church challenged the zoning decision under RFRA. The Supreme Court reiterated that Section 5 of the Fourteenth Amendment gave Congress the power to enforce existing constitutional protections, but found that this did not automatically include the power to pass any legislation to protect these rights. Instead, the Court held that there must be a "congruence and proportionality" between the injury to be remedied and the law adopted to that end. For instance, the Court's decision in *Katzenbach v. Morgan* of allowing the banning of literacy tests was justified based on an extensive history of minorities being denied suffrage in this country. In contrast, the Court found no similar pattern of the use of neutral laws of general applicability disguising religious bigotry and animus against religion. Rather than an attempt to remedy a problem, RFRA was seen by the Court as an attempt by Congress to overturn an unpopular Supreme Court decision. The law focused on no one area of alleged harm to religion, but rather just broadly inhibited state and local regulations of all types. Consequently, the Court found RFRA to be an overbroad response to a relatively nonexistent problem.

The scope of the enforcement power under Section 5 of the Fourteenth Amendment also has become important in cases where the Court has found that Congress has overreached its power under other provision of the Constitution, or is limited by some provision thereof. For instance, as discussed in detail below, the Supreme Court has held that the Eleventh Amendment and state sovereign immunity generally prohibit individuals from suing states for damages under federal law.[88] However, the Supreme Court has also held that Congress can abrogate state sovereign immunity under the Fourteenth Amendment.[89] This means that in many cases, litigants suing states will have to find a Fourteenth Amendment basis for federal legislation in order to defeat an Eleventh Amendment defense. For instance, a significant amount of federal legislation is clearly supported by the commerce clause, but it might not be supported under Section 5. Recently, the Court decided two cases that illustrate the difficulties of establishing Fourteenth Amendment authority for such legislation.

In *College Savings Bank v. Florida Prepaid Postsecondary Education Expense Board*,[90] the Supreme Court considered an unfair competition suit brought by a New Jersey savings bank against the state of Florida. The New Jersey savings bank had developed a patented program where individuals could use a certificate of deposit contract to save for college. The state of Florida set up a similar program, and the College Savings Bank sued Florida for false and misleading advertising under a provision of the Trademark Act of 1946 (Lanham Act),[91] alleging that Florida had made misleading representations about its own product.

The Court first noted that under *Seminole Tribe of Florida v. Florida*, Article I, powers such as the power to regulate commerce were insufficient to abrogate Eleventh Amendment immunity. Thus, the Court next considered whether the Lanham Act could be characterized as an exercise of Congress's power under Section 5 of the Fourteenth Amendment. Although the Fourteenth Amendment provides that no state shall "deprive a person of ... property ... without due process of law," the Court found that the unfair trade in question, which consisted of allegedly inaccurate statements made by the state of Florida about its own saving program, did not infringe on any exclusive property right held by the College Savings Bank. As the Court found that Congress had not established an authority under the Fourteenth Amendment to abrogate the state's immunity, the College Savings Bank could not proceed against the state of Florida for unfair trade practices.

Even if a property interest is established, it would still need to be determined that Congress had the authority to protect that property interest under the Fourteenth Amendment. In *Florida Prepaid Postsecondary Education Expense Board v. College Savings Bank*,[92] the Court, in a decision concerning the same parties as the case discussed above, considered whether the College Savings Bank could sue the state of Florida for patent infringement. Congress had passed a law specifically providing that states could be sued for patent violations,[93] citing three sources of constitutional authority: the Article I Patent Clause,[94] the Article I Interstate Commerce Clause,[95] and Section 5 of the Fourteenth Amendment. As the Court had previously precluded abrogation of sovereign immunity through the exercise of Article I powers, the question became whether Congress had the authority to pass patent legislation under Section 5 of the Fourteenth Amendment.

Unlike the previous case, the Court found that, under a long line of precedents, patents were considered property rights. However, the Court had to further consider whether the protection of such a property right under Section 5 of the Fourteenth Amendment was "appropriate" under its ruling in *City of Boerne*. Consequently, the Court evaluated whether a federal right to enforce patents against states was appropriate remedial or preventive legislation aimed at securing the protections of the Fourteenth Amendment for patent owners. Specifically, the Court sought to evaluate whether unremedied patent infringement by states rose to the level of a Fourteenth Amendment violation that Congress could redress.

The Court noted that Congress had failed to identify a pattern of patent infringement by the states, and that only a handful of patent infringement cases had been brought against states in the last 100 years. The Court also noted that Congress had failed to establish that state remedies for patent infringement were inadequate for citizens to seek compensation for injury. In fact, the state of Florida argued that no constitutionally based violation had occurred, as it had procedures in place that would provide the necessary due process for patent infringement by the state to be challenged. Consequently, the Court found that the exercise of Section 5 of the Fourteenth Amendment in this context would be out of proportion to the remedial objective.

The Court engaged in a similar analysis, with like results, in evaluating the application of age discrimination laws to the states. In *Kimel v. Florida Board of Regents*,[96] the Court noted that the Age Discrimination in Employment Act of 1967, while a valid exercise of Congress's commerce power, could not be applied to the states unless Congress also had the power to enact it under Section 5 of the Fourteenth Amendment. The *Kimel* Court held, however, that age is not a suspect class, and that the provisions of the ADEA far surpassed the kind of protections that would be afforded such a class under the Fourteenth Amendment. Further, the Court found that an analysis of Congress's ability to legislate prophylactically under Section 5 required an examination of the legislative record to determine whether the remedies provided were proportional and congruent to the problem. A review by the Court of the ADEA legislative record found no evidence of a pattern of state governments discriminating against employees on the basis of age. Consequently, the Court held that a state could not be liable for damages under the ADEA.

Similarly, the application of Title I of the Americans with Disabilities Act (ADA) to states was considered in the case of the *Board of Trustees v. Garrett*,[97] again with similar result. In *Garrett,* the Court evaluated whether two plaintiffs could bring claims for money damages against a state university for failing to make reasonable employment accommodations for their disabilities; one plaintiff was under treatment for cancer, the other for asthma and sleep apnea. Although disability is not a suspect class and thus discrimination is evaluated under a rational basis test, the Court had previously shown a heightened sensitivity to arbitrary discrimination against the disabled.[98] Further, Congress had made substantial findings regarding the pervasiveness of such discrimination. However, the Supreme Court declined to consider evidence of discrimination by either the private sector or local government, and dismissed the examples that did relate to the states as unlikely to rise to the level of constitutionally "irrational" discrimination. Ultimately, the Court found that no pattern of unconstitutional state discrimination against the disabled had been established, and that the application of the ADA was not a proportionate response to any pattern that might exist.

However, the Court reached a different conclusion in the case of *Nevada Department of Human Resources v. Hibbs*.[99] In the *Hibbs* case, an employee of the Nevada Department of Human Resources had a dispute with the Department regarding how much leave time he had available under the Family and Medical Leave Act of 1993 (FMLA). The FMLA requires employers to provide employees up to 12 weeks of unpaid leave to care for a close relative with a "serious health condition."[100] In *Hibbs*, the Court held that Congress had the power to abrogate a state's Eleventh Amendment immunity under the FMLA, so that a state employee could recover money damages. The Court found that Congress had established significant evidence of a long and extensive history of sex discrimination with respect to the administration of leave benefits by the states, and that history was sufficient to justify the enactment of the legislation under Section 5. The standard for demonstrating the constitutionality of a gender-based classification is more difficult to meet than the rational-basis test, such was at issue in *Kimel* and *Garrett*, so it was easier for Congress to show a pattern of state constitutional violations.

Even where the Eleventh Amendment and state sovereign immunity are not at issue, the Court may be asked to consider whether the Fourteenth Amendment establishes a sufficient basis for a federal law that does not appear to have a constitutional basis elsewhere in the Constitution. For instance, in *United States v. Morrison*,[101] discussed previously,[102] the Court found that Congress, in creating a federal private right of action for victims of gender-motivated violence, had exceeded its authority under the Commerce Clause. Consequently, the plaintiff in that case made the alternate argument that the federal private right of action could be sustained under Section 5 of the Fourteenth Amendment.

This argument, however, suffered from two major defects. First, the Court has long held that the Fourteenth Amendment provides Congress with the authority to regulate states but not individuals.[103] In *Morrison*, however, the civil case had been brought against the individuals alleged to have engaged in the offense. The plaintiff attempted to avoid this problem by arguing that there is pervasive bias in various state justice systems against victims of gender-motivated violence, and that providing a federal private right of action was an appropriate means to remedy this "state action."

However, the Court rejected this argument, finding that the remedy did not meet the *City of Boerne* test of "congruence and proportionality to the injury to be prevented or remedied and the means adopted to that end."[104] Because the federal private right of action was not aimed at the allegedly discriminatory actions by state officials, but was instead directed against the individual engaging in the violence itself, the Court found that the action could not be supported by reference to the Fourteenth Amendment.[105]

The Court again considered the issue of Congress's power under Section 5 of the Fourteenth Amendment in *Tennessee v. Lane.*[106] In the *Lane* case, two paraplegic plaintiffs alleged that the state of Tennessee and several of its counties violated Title II of the ADA, which requires that the disabled be provided access to public services, programs, and activities, by failing to provide physical access to state courts.[107] The Court held that Title II, as applied to this right of access to the courts, was a proper exercise of Congress's authority under Section 5 of the Fourteenth Amendment to abrogate states' Eleventh Amendment immunity. Similar to its holdings in the *Garrett* and *Hibbs* cases, the Court found that Congress had established sufficient evidence of the sustained denial of persons with disabilities of access to the courts.[108]

In applying the *Boerne* congruence and proportionality test, the Court in *Lane* distinguished the rights Congress intended to protect in Title II (access to public services, programs, and activities) from the Title I employment rights that had been struck down in *Garrett.* While both Titles I and II were intended to address unequal treatment of the disabled (which is only a constitutional violation when it is irrational), the Court held that Title II was also intended to reach the more rigorously protected rights of the Due Process Clause of the Fourteenth Amendment, such as the right of access to the courts.[109] The Court stated that the due process rights Congress sought to protect under Title II required a standard of judicial review at least as searching as the sex-based classifications the Court considered in *Hibbs*.[110] The limited nature of Title II as a remedy for the denial of the right of access to courts also informed the Court's holding that the measure is a valid prophylactic remedy.[111]

Congress's authority under Section 5 of the Fourteenth Amendment to abrogate states' Eleventh Amendment immunity appears strongest when the focus of the prophylactic measure at issue is conduct that actually violates a constitutional right. In *United States v. Georgia*,[112] a disabled state prison inmate who used a wheelchair for mobility alleged that the state of Georgia violated Title II of the ADA in relation to his conditions of confinement. The Court reiterated its holding in *Lane* that Title II is a constitutional exercise of Congress's Fourteenth Amendment powers. It went on to state that Title II was valid as applied to the plaintiff's cause of action, because he alleged independent violations under Section 1 of the Fourteenth Amendment concerning his prison treatment.[113]

THE TENTH AMENDMENT

The Tenth Amendment provides that "powers not delegated to the United States by the Constitution, nor prohibited by it to the States, are reserved to the States respectively, or to the people." While this language would appear to represent one of the most clear examples of a federalist principle in the Constitution, it has not had a significant impact in limiting federal powers. Initially, the Supreme Court interpreted the Tenth Amendment to have substantive content, so that certain "core" state functions would be beyond the authority of the federal government to regulate. Thus, in *National League of Cities v. Usery*,[114] the Court struck down federal wage and price controls on state employees as involving the regulation of core state functions.[115] The Court, however, overruled *National League of Cities* in *Garcia v. San Antonio Metropolitan Transit Authority*.[116] In sum, the Court in *Garcia* seems to have said that most disputes over the effects on state sovereignty of federal commerce power legislation are to be considered political questions, and that the states should look for relief from federal regulation through the political process.[117] This appeared to have ended the Court's attempt to substantively limit federal government regulation of the states.

The Court soon turned, however, to the question of how the Constitution limits the process by which the federal government regulates the states. In *New York v. United States*,[118] Congress had attempted to regulate in the area of low-level radioactive waste. In a 1985 statute, Congress provided that states must either develop legislation on how to dispose of all low-level radioactive waste generated within the state, or the state would be forced to take title to such waste, which would mean that it became the state's responsibility. The Court found that although Congress had the authority under the Commerce Clause to regulate low-level radioactive waste, it only had the power to regulate the waste directly. Here, Congress had attempted to require the states to perform the regulation, and decreed that the failure to do so would require the state to deal with the financial consequences of owning large quantities of radioactive waste. In effect, Congress sought to "commandeer" the legislative process of the states. In the *New York* case, the Court found that this power was not found in the text or structure of the Constitution, and it was thus a violation of the Tenth Amendment.

A later case presented the question of the extent to which Congress could regulate through a state's executive branch officers. This case, *Printz v. United States*,[119] involved the Brady Handgun Act. The Brady Handgun Act required state and local law-enforcement officers to conduct background checks on prospective handgun purchasers within five business days of an attempted purchase. This portion of the act was challenged under the Tenth Amendment, under the theory that Congress was without authority to "commandeer" state executive branch officials. After a historical study of federal commandeering of state officials, the Court concluded that commandeering of state executive branch officials was, like commandeering of the legislature, outside of Congress's power, and consequently a violation of the Tenth Amendment.

Although the federal government is prohibited from commandeering either the legislature or executive branch of a state, this does not appear to be the case with state judicial branches. The federal judicial system and the state judicial system were not intended to be as separate as the other branches of government, and the Supremacy Clause of the Constitution explicitly provides that state courts must follow federal law, even if it overrides state laws or constitutions.[120] So, there appears to be less of a concern regarding the "commandeering" of state courts.

A key distinction between constitutional "substantive regulation" and unconstitutional "commandeering" appears to be whether or not the federal mandate in question is regulating state activities or whether it is seeking to control the manner in which states regulate private parties. Thus, for instance, the Court recently held in *Reno v. Condon*[121] that the Driver's Privacy Protection Act of 1994, which regulates the sale of personal information gathered from persons seeking driver's licenses, was substantive regulation, not commandeering. In that case, the Court found that the state was not being directed on how to regulate its citizens, but rather on how to treat information that had been elicited from those citizens. However, because the regulation affected both state governments and private resellers of such information, the Court reserved the question as to whether a law, which only regulated state activities, would be constitutionally suspect.

ELEVENTH AMENDMENT AND STATE SOVEREIGN IMMUNITY

The Eleventh Amendment and state sovereign immunity provide an example of the complicated interaction between the powers of the federal government, the state, and the individual. The basic issue to be addressed here is the extent to which individuals can sue a state under federal law.[122] The answer to this question may vary based on a number of factors, including what law the suit is being brought under, whether the state has taken action to make itself amenable to such law, and what relief is being sought.

The starting point for such a discussion is usually the Eleventh Amendment. The Eleventh Amendment reads, in part, as follows: "The Judicial power of the United States shall not be construed to extend to any suit in law or equity, commenced or prosecuted against one of the United States by Citizens of another State." The actual text of the Amendment appears to be limited to preventing U.S. or foreign citizens from bringing diversity cases against states in federal courts. However, the Supreme Court has expanded the concept of state sovereign immunity to reach much further than the text of the amendment.

The Eleventh Amendment, the first amendment to the Constitution after the adoption of the Bill of Rights, was passed as a response to the case of *Chisholm v. Georgia*.[123] Immediately after the adoption of the Constitution, a number of citizens filed cases in federal court against states. One of these, *Chisholm*, was a diversity suit filed by two citizens of South Carolina against the State of Georgia to recover a Revolutionary War debt. In *Chisholm,* the Supreme Court noted that Article III of the Constitution specifically grants the federal courts diversity jurisdiction over suits "between a State and citizens of another State."[124] Thus, the Court held that this grant of jurisdiction authorized the private citizen of one state to sue another state in federal court without that state's consent.

The states were outraged that such a suit could be brought in federal court, protesting that the drafters of the Constitution had promised the states they would not be sued by their debtors in federal courts. Almost immediately after the decision of the *Chisholm* cases, resolutions were introduced in Congress to overturn it, the end result being the Eleventh Amendment. The amendment ensured that a citizen of one state could not sue another state in federal court—in other words, a citizen could not sue under federal diversity jurisdiction without a state's permission.

However, even after the Eleventh Amendment was passed, a number of cases were filed against states by private citizens, with jurisdiction based on federal question rather than diversity. Under this reasoning, if a citizen of a state sued his or her own state in federal court, the prohibition of the Eleventh Amendment would not apply. Consequently, for a number of years after the passage of the Eleventh Amendment, this type of case was entertained by the federal courts. However, this line of cases was ended by the case of *Hans v. Louisiana*.[125]

In *Hans v. Louisiana*, the Court provided for an interpretation of the Eleventh Amendment that allowed the Court to move beyond the literal text of that amendment. Under the reasoning of the Court, the Eleventh Amendment was not so much an amendment to the original structure of the Constitution as it was an attempt to overturn a specific court decision that had misinterpreted this structure. According to this line of reasoning, the Eleventh Amendment was not an amendment, but a restoration of the original constitutional design.

Ultimately, the issue before the Court in *Hans v. Louisiana* and in subsequent cases was not the Eleventh Amendment, but the issue of state sovereign immunity. State sovereign immunity means that a state must consent to be sued in its own court system. This concept is based on early English law, which provided that the Crown could not be sued in English courts without its consent. The doctrine of sovereign immunity was in effect in the states that were in existence at the time of the drafting of the Constitution. Further, various writings by the founding fathers seemed to support the concept.[126] Thus, the issue before the Court in *Hans* was whether the grant of jurisdiction to federal courts under Article III of the Constitution had abrogated state sovereign immunity. The *Hans* Court found that Article III did not have this effect.

Although the *Hans* Court answered the issue of whether adoption of Article III of the Constitution had waived state sovereign immunity in federal courts, it left a number of questions unanswered. For instance, the question as to whether there are any instances where Congress could, by statute, abrogate a state's sovereign immunity, so that a citizen could sue a state under federal law. In *Seminole Tribe of Florida v. Florida,*[127] the Court seemed to answer that in most cases, such suits would not be accepted. The *Seminole* case involved the Indian Gaming Regulatory Act of 1988, which provided Indian tribes with an opportunity to establish gambling operations. However, to establish such gambling, the Indian tribes had to enter into a compact with the state in which they were located. The states, in turn, were obligated to negotiate with the Indian tribes in good faith, and this requirement was made enforceable in federal court. Thus, the question arose as to whether the tribes could sue the states under the Eleventh Amendment.

The Court in *Seminole* found it important to establish what constitutional authority was being exercised by the passage of the Indian Gaming Law. The Court determined that the power being exercised was the Indian Commerce Clause,[128] which is found in Article I. The Court had found previously in *Pennsylvania v. Union Gas*,[129] that the Commerce Power, as a plenary power, was so broad that of necessity it required the ability to abrogate state sovereign immunity. In *Seminole*, however, the Court overturned *Union Gas*, holding that as the Eleventh Amendment was ratified after the passage of the Constitution and Article I, it was a limitation on Congress's authority to waive a state's sovereign immunity under that Article. The Court did indicate, however, that Congress can abrogate state sovereignty under the Fourteenth Amendment. While the logic behind this distinction is unclear,[130] it means that in many cases, litigants suing states will try to find a Fourteenth Amendment basis for federal legislation to defeat an Eleventh Amendment defense.

A question left unanswered by the *Hans* decision was whether the Eleventh Amendment, which prohibited Congress from abrogating a state's sovereign immunity in federal court, extended to a state's own courts. In *Alden v. Maine*,[131] the Supreme Court found that the same principles of sovereign immunity identified in *Hans* would prevent Congress from authorizing a state to be sued in its own courts without permission. As in *Hans*, the Court acknowledged that the literal text of the Eleventh Amendment does not prohibit such suits, as its language addresses only suits brought in federal courts. Consequently, the Court relied instead on the proposition that sovereign immunity is a "fundamental postulate" of the constitutional design, and is not amenable to congressional abrogation. The same reasoning that prohibited these suits from being brought in federal court, a deference to the "respect and dignity" of state sovereignty, led the Court to conclude that it would be anomalous to allow such cases to be brought instead in state court.

In *Federal Maritime Comm'n v. South Carolina State Ports Authority*, the Court addressed the issue of whether state sovereign immunity extended to proceedings before federal agencies.[132] In this case, the South Carolina State Ports Authority denied a cruise ship permission to berth at the state's port facilities in Charleston, South Carolina, contending that the primary purpose of the cruise was for gambling. The cruise ship company, Maritime Services, filed a claim with the Federal Maritime Commission (FMC) arguing that South Carolina had discriminated against it in violation of the Shipping Act of 1984 and sought, among other things, damages for loss of profits.[133] The Port

Authority, however, successfully moved to dismiss the complaint, arguing that it was inconsistent with the concept of state sovereign immunity.

In reviewing the case, the Court analogized between the FMC's quasi-judicial proceedings and traditional judicial proceedings, while noting that "[t]he preeminent purpose of state sovereign immunity is to accord States the dignity that is consistent with their status as sovereign entities."[134] Consequently, the Court agreed that state sovereign immunity bars the FMC from adjudicating damage claims made by a private party against a nonconsenting state.[135] In dissent, however, Justice Breyer noted that agency administrative proceedings are not judicial proceedings and that the ultimate enforcement of such proceedings in a court is done by the federal agency, to which state sovereign immunity does not apply. Thus, while an agency remains capable of enforcement actions against states in federal court, it cannot use its own adjudicative process to determine whether to do so, but must rely on its investigatory powers.[136] According to Justice Breyer, "[t]he natural result is less agency flexibility, a larger federal bureaucracy, less fair procedure, and potentially less effective law enforcement."[137]

THE SPENDING CLAUSE

It should be noted that in many instances, the federal government still has the ability to influence state behavior despite the constitutional limits discussed above.[138] One of the more significant ways that the federal government can encourage state behavior is to impose conditions on the receipt of federal monies by the states. Considering the large amount of funds provided to states by the federal government, this represents a significant power for Congress to exercise. Further, as the concept of grant conditioning can involve waiver by the states of Tenth Amendment rights, these grant conditions may allow Congress to indirectly achieve compliance by a state in a way that could not be achieved directly.

The question of whether a state can be required to perform (or refrain from) certain actions was addressed in the Supreme Court case of *South Dakota v. Dole*.[139] In *Dole*, Congress enacted the National Minimum Drinking Age Amendment of 1984,[140] which directed the Secretary of Transportation to withhold a percentage of federal highway funds from states in which the age for purchase of alcohol was below 21 years. The state of South Dakota, which permitted 19-year-olds to purchase beer, brought suit arguing that the law was an invalid exercise of Congress's power under the Spending Clause to provide for the "general welfare."[141] The Supreme Court held that, as the indirect imposition of such a standard was directed toward the general welfare of the country, it was a valid exercise of Congress's spending power.

The Court noted that the grant condition did not implicate an independent constitutional bar (i.e., the grant condition did not require the state to engage in an unconstitutional activity). Further, the court noted that the grant condition was not a violation of the Tenth Amendment, which generally prevents Congress from "commandeering" state legislatures[142] and executive branch officials[143] to implement federal programs.[144] The Tenth Amendment would not apply here, the Court held, because the state officials were voluntarily cooperating in order to receive federal grants, and thus were not being directed to comply with federal mandates.

The Court did suggest, however, that there were limits to Congress's power under the Spending Clause. First, a grant condition must be related to the particular national projects or programs to which the money was being directed.[145] In *Dole*, the congressional condition imposing a specific drinking age was found to be related to the national concern of safe interstate travel, which was one of the main purposes for highway funds being expended. Second, the Court suggested that, in some circumstances, the financial inducements offered by Congress might be so coercive as to pass the point at which "pressure turns into compulsion,"[146] which would suggest a violation of the Tenth Amendment. In *Dole*, however, the percentage of highway funds that were to be withheld from a state with a drinking age below 21 was relatively small, so that Congress's program did not coerce the states to enact higher minimum drinking ages than they would otherwise choose.

The case of *National Federation of Independent Business (NFIB) v. Sebelius*,[147] however, seemed to suggest that an alternative line of analysis might apply in some grant condition cases. In 2010, Congress passed the Patient Protection and Affordable Care Act (ACA).[148] The ACA, among other things, required states to expand Medicaid eligibility or lose Medicaid funding. Following the enactment of the ACA, state attorneys general and others brought several lawsuits challenging various provisions of the act on constitutional grounds. The Supreme Court, in a controlling opinion by Chief Justice Roberts,[149] found that the enforcement mechanism for the ACA Medicaid expansion, withdrawal of all Medicaid funds, was a violation of the Tenth Amendment.[150]

As noted in *Dole*, the loss of federal funds associated with a grant condition cannot be so large that the withholding of such funds is coercive. Justice Roberts's opinion in *NFIB*, however, addressed the slightly different question of whether a grant condition attached to a "new and independent" program (here, the Medicaid expansion) that threatened the funding of an existing program (here, Medicaid) violated the Tenth Amendment. It is unclear, therefore, whether the *NFIB* decision was an application of the *Dole* analysis, or whether the combination of factors presented in *NFIB* suggests an alternate line of reasoning.[151]

Justice Roberts's opinion in *NFIB* held that, in the case of existing program funding being conditioned on the adoption of a "new and independent" program, the amount of federal funds at issue cannot represent a significant portion of a state's budget or its withdrawal will be found to be unconstitutionally coercive under the Tenth Amendment. Justice Roberts did not identify a standard to determine what level of withholding funds would be coercive, or specify what kind of distinguishing factors were necessary to such analysis. He did conclude, however, that withdrawal of federal program funds which made up 10% of an average state's budget represented a "gun to the head" and was a form of "economic dragooning."[152]

It is not clear, however, whether the confluence of factors at issue in the *NFIB* case is likely to be present in future cases. Few federal programs, for instance, even approach the level of state funding as does Medicaid; nor do there appear to be significant examples of grant conditions requiring creation of "new and independent" programs in order to retain funding for a separate program. Consequently, the *NFIB* case may have minimal effect on the validity of existing or future federal grant conditions.

CONCLUSION

It would appear that the status of the state in the federal system has been strengthened by recent Supreme Court opinions. Although the Court has not scaled back the federal government's substantive jurisdiction significantly, it has to some extent prevented the expansion of Congress's power under the Commerce Clause and under Section 5 of the Fourteenth Amendment. Further it has created a variety of obstacles as to how these powers can be executed, forbidding Congress under the Tenth Amendment from commandeering the authority of state legislative and executive branches, and limiting the authority of Congress to abrogate state sovereign immunity.

Ultimately, however, Congress retains significant powers to influence state behavior, such as through the Spending Clause, and, under the

Supremacy Clause, Congress may require the enforcement of its laws in both state and federal court.

End Notes

[1] Portions of this report were prepared by Kristin Thornblad, legal intern.

[2] See, e.g., U.S. Const. Art. I, §10, cl. 2 ("No State shall ... lay any Imposts or Duties on Imports or Exports.")

[3] "No State shall, without the Consent of Congress, lay any Duty of Tonnage, keep Troops, or Ships of War in time of Peace, enter into any Agreement or Compact with another State, or with a foreign Power, or engage in War, unless actually invaded, or in such imminent Danger as will not admit of delay." U.S. Const., Art. I, §10, cl. 3.

[4] "Full Faith and Credit shall be given in each State to the public Acts, Records, and Judicial Proceedings of every other State. And the Congress may by general Laws prescribe the Manner in which such Acts, Records, and Proceedings shall be proved, and the Effect thereof." U.S. Const. Art. IV, §1. This "Full Faith and Credit Clause" gives Congress what amounts to enforcement authority over the required recognition by each state of the judgments, records, and legislation of other states.

[5] "... [N]o new State shall be formed or erected within the Jurisdiction of any other State; nor any State be formed by the Junction of two or more States, or parts of States, without the Consent of the Legislatures of the States concerned as well as of the Congress." U.S. Const., Art. IV, §3, cl. 1.

[6] Gibbons v. Ogden, 22 U.S. (9 Wheat.) 1 (1824).

[7] Article I, Section 1, of the Constitution provides that "All legislative powers herein granted shall be vested in a Congress of the United States." Unlike a typical grant of power to states Article I, Section 1, does not grant to Congress "all legislative power," but rather grants to Congress only those specific powers enumerated in Section 8 and elsewhere in the Constitution.

[8] As stated by Chief Justice Marshall in McCulloch v. Maryland, 17 U.S. (4 Wheat.) 316 (1819): "Let the end be legitimate, let it be within the scope of the Constitution, and all means which are appropriate, which are plainly adapted to that end, which are not prohibited, but consist with the letter and spirit of the Constitution, are constitutional."

[9] "The Congress shall have Power To lay and collect Taxes, Duties, Imposts and Excises, to pay the Debts and provide for the common Defence and general Welfare of the United States; but all Duties, Imposts and Excises shall be uniform throughout the United States." U.S. Const., Art. I, §8, cl. 1.

[10] "No Money shall be drawn from the Treasury, but in Consequence of Appropriations made by Law." U.S. Const., Art. I, §9, cl. 7.

[11] United States v. Butler, 297 U.S. 1 (1936).

[12] "To regulate commerce with foreign Nations, and among the several States, and with the Indian Tribes." U.S. Const., Article I, §8, cl. 3.

[13] U.S. Const., Art. I, §8, cl. 4.

[14] U.S. Const., Art. I, §8 cl. 5.

[15] U.S. Const., Art. I, §8, cl. 6.

[16] U.S. Const., Art. I, §8, cl. 7.

17 U.S. Const., Art. I, §8, cl. 8.

[18] "The Congress shall have power ... To establish an uniform Rule of Naturalization." U.S. Const., Art I, §8, cl. 4. "All persons born or naturalized in the United States and subject to the jurisdiction thereof, are citizens of the United States and of the State wherein they reside." U.S. Const., Amend. XIV, §1.

[19] "No State shall make or enforce any law which shall abridge the privileges or immunities of citizens of the United States; nor shall any State deprive any person of life, liberty, or property, without due process of law; nor deny to any person within its jurisdiction the equal protection of the laws." U.S. Const., Amend. XIV, §1. The Congress shall have power to enforce, by appropriate legislation, the provisions of this article. Id. at §5.

[20] U.S. Const., Amend. XXVI.

[21] U.S. Const., Amend. XV.

[22] U.S. Const., Amend. XIX.

[23] "The Times, Places and Manner of holding Elections for Senators and Representatives, shall be prescribed in each State by the Legislature thereof; but the Congress may at any time by Law make or alter such Regulations, except as to the Places of chusing Senators." U.S. Const., Article I, §4, cl. 1. While the Fifteenth Amendment and the other voting rights guarantees noted above protect only against state action, congressional authority under this clause includes protection of the electoral process against private interference. A variety of enactments can be traced to this authority, including campaign finance laws and the Hatch Act (insofar as it applies to federal elections).

[24] "Each House shall be the Judge of the Elections, Returns and Qualifications of its own Members." Article I, §5, cl. 1. The House and the Senate act as judicial tribunals in resolving contested election cases.

[25] See, e.g., U.S. Const., Amend. XIV, §2 (apportionment).

[26] "The Congress shall have power ... To exercise exclusive Legislation in all Cases whatsoever, over such District ... as may, by Cession of Particular States, and the Acceptance of Congress, become the Seat of the Government of the United States, and to exercise like Authority over all Places purchased by the Consent of the Legislature of the State in which the Same shall be, for the Erection of Forts, Magazines, Arsenals, dock-Yards and other needful Buildings." Article I, §8, cl. 17. "The Congress shall have power to dispose of and make all needful Rules and Regulations respecting the Territory or other Property belonging to the United States.... " Article IV, §3, cl. 2.

[27] "[N]or shall private property be taken for public use, without just compensation." U.S. Const., Amend. V. Implicit in the Fifth Amendment's requirement that just compensation be paid for private property that is taken for a public use is the existence of the government's power to take private property for public use.

[28] See, e.g., U.S. Const. Art. I, §8, cl. 10 ("The Congress shall have power ... To define and punish Piracies and Felonies committed on the high Seas, and Offences against the Law of Nations"); U.S. Const., Art. I, §8, cl. 11 ("... To declare War, grant Letters of Marque and Reprisal, and make Rules concerning Captures on Land and Water."); U.S. Const., Art. I, §8, cl. 12 ("To raise and support Armies.... ").

[29] U.S. Const., Art. I, §8, cl. 3.

[30] 514 U.S. 549 (1995).

[31] 18 U.S.C. §922(q)(1)A).

[32] Abel, The Commerce Clause in the Constitutional Convention and in Contemporary Comment, 25 Minn. L. Rev. 432, 443-44 (1941); Greenspan, The Constitutional Exercise of the Federal Police Power: A Functional Approach to Federalism, 41 Vanderbilt Law Review 1019, 1022-24 (1988). Those materials which do address congressional control over

commerce focus on the necessity of uniformity in matters of foreign commerce, although the drafters clearly intended domestic commerce to be regulated as well. P. Kurland & R. Lerner, THE FOUNDER'S CONSTITUTION 477-528 (1987).

[33] Alexander Hamilton, CONTINENTALIST, No. 5, 18 April 1782 (Paper 3:75-82) as reprinted in P. Kurland & R. Lerner, supra note 32 ("The vesting of the power of regulating trade ought to have been a principal object of the confederation for a variety of reasons. It is as necessary for the purposes of commerce as of revenue.")

[34] Greenspan, supra note 32 at 1023.

[35] Gibbons v. Odgen, 22 U.S. (9 Wheat.) 1, 197-98 (1824).

[36] See, e.g., Brown v. Maryland, 25 U.S. (12 Wheat.) 419 (1827).

[37] United States v. Lopez, 514 U.S. at 593 (Thomas, J., dissenting).

[38] Champion v. Ames (The Lottery Case), 188 U.S. 321 (1903).

[39] Hippolite Egg Co. v. United States, 220 U.S. 45 (1911).

[40] Hoke v. United States, 227 U.S. 308 (1913).

[41] United States v. E.C. Knight Co., 156 U.S. 1, 12 (1895).

[42] Carter v. Carter Coal Co., 298 U.S. 238, 304 (1936).

[43] 301 U.S. 1 (1937).

[44] 301 U.S. at 41.

[45] United States v. Darby, 312 U.S. 100 (1941)(approving legislation relating to working conditions).

[46] 312 U.S. at 121.

[47] Wickard v. Filburn, 317 U.S. 111 (1942).

[48] Id.

[49] See Heart of Atlanta Motel v. United States, 370 U.S. 241 (1964); Katzenbach v. McClung, 379 U.S. 241 (1964).

[50] Perez v. United States, 402 U.S. 146 (1971).

[51] Herman Schwartz, Court Tries to Patrol a Political Line, Legal Times 25 (May 8, 1995).

[52] The Court failed to note that to some extent, the three categories are intertwined. For instance, the first category, the regulation of "streams" or "channels" of commerce, allows regulation of the creation, movement, sale and consumption of merchandise or services. But the initial extension of the "streams" of commerce analysis by the Court to intrastate trade was justified by the "effect" of these other activities on commerce. See NLRB v. Jones & Laughlin, 301 U.S. 1, 31 (1936). Similarly, the second category, which allows the regulation of such instrumentalities of commerce as planes, trains or trucks, is also based on the theory that a threat to these instrumentalities "affects" commerce, even if the effect is local in nature. Southern Railway Company v. United States, 222 U.S. 21, 26-27 (1911)(regulation of intrastate rail traffic has a substantial effect on interstate rail traffic). Thus, the final category identified by the Court appears to be a catch-all for all other activities which "substantially affect" commerce.

[53] 514 U.S. at 559.

[54] Wickard v. Filburn, 317 U.S. 111 (1942).

[55] 514 U.S. at 564. The Court rejected arguments that possession of guns in school affected the national economy by its negative impact on education. Id.

[56] 514 U.S. at 561.

[57] 514 U.S. at 560.

[58] 514 U.S. at 580 (Kennedy, J., concurring). The Court has reiterated its concern over extending Commerce Clause powers to Congress in areas of the law traditionally reserved to the states. See, e.g., Solid Waste Agency of Northern Cook County (SWANCC) v. U.S. Army

Corps of Engineers, 531 U.S. 159, 174 (2001) (rejecting an interpretation of the Clean Water Act which allowed regulation of nonnavigable, isolated wetlands as infringing upon the "traditional and primary state power over land and water use").

[59] See, e.g., 18 U.S.C. §247 (2000)(forbidding obstruction of persons in the free exercise of religious beliefs where the offense "is in or affects interstate or foreign commerce.")

[60] 529 U.S. 598 (2000).

[61] Id. at 609.

[62] The requirement that a commerce clause regulation be economic or commercial has been influential in a number of subsequent statutory interpretation cases. In Jones v. United States, 529 U.S. 848 (2000), a criminal defendant challenged his conviction under 18 U.S.C. Section 844(i), which, in part, makes it a crime to destroy by fire or explosive a building "used" in interstate commerce. Applying the statutory canon that one should interpret a statute to avoid constitutional doubt, Jones v. United States, 526 U.S. 227, 239 (1999), the Court held that the statute did not apply to a private residence that was "used" as collateral to obtain and secure a loan, "used" to obtain insurance, and "used" to receive natural gas from other sources. The Court construed the statute to require that a building protected by Section 844(i) be "actively employed" for commercial purposes, id. at 855, arguing that a broader interpretation would extend the statute to virtually every arson in the country.
A similar result occurred in the case of Solid Waste Agency of Northern Cook County (SWANCC) v. U.S. Army Corps of Engineers, 531 U.S. 159 (2001). In SWANCC, the Court considered a challenge to the Migratory Bird Rule, 51 Fed. Reg. 41217, which extended Section 404(a) of the Clean Water Act (CWA), 33 U.S.C. §1344(a) to nonnavigable, isolated wetlands. The Court held that this interpretation of the statute would raise serious constitutional questions, requiring, for instance, a close examination of precisely what activity was being regulated. Absent a clear statement from Congress that it intended the Clean Water Act to have such a broad reach, the Court found the rule was not supported by the statute. Id. at 173. See also Rapanos v. United States Army Corps of Engineers, 165 L. Ed. 2d 159, 201 (2006).

[63] 545 U.S. 1 (2005).

[64] Cal. Health & Safety Code Ann §11362.5 (West Supp. 2005) (providing for the legal possession of medical marijuana by a patient or primary caregiver, upon the written or oral recommendation of a physician).

[65] 545 U.S. at 28.

[66] 317 U.S. 111 (1942).

[67] Id. at 125.

[68] 52 Stat. 31.

[69] Id. at 128-29.

[70] Id. at 127.

[71] 545 U.S. at 19.

[72] Id.

[73] U.S. Const., Art. I, §8, cl. 18.

[74] 545 U.S. at 22.

[75] (Scalia, J., concurring) (citations omitted).

[76] Art. I, Section 8, cl. 1 provides that "The Congress shall have Power to lay and collect Taxes, Duties, Imposts and Excises, to pay the Debts and provide for the common Defence and general Welfare of the United States; but all Duties, Imposts and Excises shall be uniform throughout the United States."

[77] 541 U.S. 600 (2004).

[78] 541 U.S. at 606.
[79] No. 08–1224 slip. op. (May 17, 2010).
[80] Id. at 22.
[81] 4 Wheat. 316, 421 (1819).
[82] U.S. Const., Amend. XIII (prohibiting slavery).
[83] U.S. Const., Amend. XV (voting rights).
[84] 384 U.S. 641 (1966).
[85] 400 U.S. 112 (1970).
[86] 521 U.S. 507 (1997).
[87] 494 U.S. 872 (1990).
[88] See notes 90-104 and accompanying text, infra.
[89] Seminole Tribe of Florida v. Florida, 517 U.S. 44, 65-66 (1996); See discussion infra notes 95-98 and accompanying text.
[90] 527 U.S. 666 (1999).
[91] 15 U.S.C. §1125(a).
[92] 527 U.S. 627 (1999).
[93] Patent and Plant Variety Protection Remedy Clarification Act (Patent Remedy Act), 35 U.S.C. §§271(a).
[94] U.S. Const. Art. I, §8, cl. 8.
[95] U.S. Const. Art. I, §8, cl. 3.
[96] 528 U.S. 62 (2000).
[97] 531 U.S. 356 (2001).
[98] Cleburne v. Cleburne Living Center, Inc., 473 U.S. 432 (1985).
[99] 538 U.S. 721 (2003).
[100] 29 U.S.C. §2612(a)(1)(C).
[101] 529 U.S. 598 (2000).
[102] See supra notes 60-61 and accompanying text.
[103] See Shelley v. Kraemer, 334 U.S. 1, 13 (1948).
[104] 521 U.S. at 526.
[105] 529 U.S. at 626.
[106] 541 U.S. 509 (2004).
[107] One plaintiff in Lane claimed he was unable to appear to answer criminal charges on the second floor of a courthouse that had no elevator. The second plaintiff, a certified court reporter, claimed she was denied the opportunity both to work and to participate in the judicial process because she was unable to access numerous county courthouses.
[108] The Court cited congressional evidence that legislative attempts preceding Title II inadequately addressed the problem of patterned unconstitutional treatment in access to the courts. 541 U.S. at 526.
[109] The Court held that it need not examine Title II as a whole when evaluating the remedy's congruence and proportionality to the injury of disability discrimination in access to the courts. The relevant inquiry solely concerned Title II's scope as applied to the rights associated with access to judicial services. The Court cited as precedent for this limited application approach the Garrett case, in which it considered only Title I of the ADA for purposes of Fourteenth Amendment analysis. Based on this narrow scope of inquiry, the Court determined that both the pattern of past discrimination in access to the courts and the failure of previous legislative attempts to remedy the injury were sufficient to hold that Title II is a valid exercise of Congress's power under Section 5 of the Fourteenth Amendment.

[110] 541 U.S. at 529. As noted by Chief Justice Rehnquist in dissent, 541 U.S. at 541-42 (Rehnquist, C.J., dissenting), the congruence and proportionality analysis in the majority opinion in Lane did not limit itself to historical examples of the disabled being denied due process, but also cited a history of disparate treatment in other less protected areas. See id. at 524-25.

[111] Title II does not require states to compromise the integrity of public programs or make unduly burdensome changes to public facilities. 541 U.S. at 532. Rather, states need only take reasonable measures to comply with Title II regulations. Id.

[112] 546 U.S. 151 (2006).

[113] Id. at 157.

[114] 426 U.S. 833 (1976).

[115] In National League of Cities v. Usery, the Court conceded that the legislation under attack, which regulated the wages and hours of certain state and local governmental employees, was undoubtedly within the scope of the Commerce Clause, but it cautioned that there are attributes of sovereignty attaching to every state government which may not be impaired by Congress, not because Congress may lack an affirmative grant of legislative authority to reach the matter, but because the Constitution prohibits it from exercising the authority in that manner.

[116] 469 U.S. 528 (1985). Justice Blackmun's opinion for the Court in Garcia concluded that the National League of Cities test for "integral operations" in areas of traditional governmental functions had proven impractical, and that the Court in 1976 had "tried to repair what did not need repair."

[117] See also South Carolina v. Baker, 485 U.S. 505 (1988).

[118] 505 U.S. 144 (1992).

[119] 521 U.S. 898 (1997).

[120] "The Constitution and the Laws of the United States ... shall be the Supreme Law of the Land; and the Judges in every State shall be bound thereby.... " U.S. Const., Art. VI, cl. 2.

[121] 528 U.S. 141 (2000).

[122] It should be noted that not all suits in which a state is involved is a "suit" against a state. In Tennessee Student Assistance Corp. v. Hood, 541 U.S. 440 (2004), the Court addressed state sovereign immunity in the context of bankruptcy proceedings. In that case, the Court addressed whether Eleventh Amendment immunity extended to an adversary proceeding initiated by a debtor seeking an undue hardship discharge of her state-held student loan debt. The Court held that the proceeding did not constitute a suit against the state for purposes of the Eleventh Amendment. The Court noted that the bankruptcy petition in question was an in rem proceeding, so that the court's jurisdiction was over the petitioner's debt, rather than over her person or the state. Id. at 448. Thus, the federal bankruptcy court's exercise of jurisdiction over the state-held debt did not infringe upon the state's sovereignty immunity. Id. at 450.

[123] 2 U.S. (Dall.) 419 (1793).

[124] U.S. Const., Art. III, §2.

[125] 134 U.S. 1 (1890).

[126] See Alden v. Maine, 527 U.S. 706, 2248 (1999).

[127] 517 U.S. 44 (1996).

[128] U.S. Const., Art. I, §8, cl. 3.

[129] 491 U.S. 1 (1989).

[130] One apparent argument is that the Fourteenth Amendment was passed after the Eleventh Amendment and thus, unlike legislative powers found in Article I of the Constitution, it can

be seen as an alteration of the restrictions of the Eleventh Amendment. Seminole Tribe of Florida v. Florida, 517 U.S. 44, 65-66 (1996). However, as is discussed in detail below, the Supreme Court has held that state sovereign immunity preceded and predated the Constitution. Alden v. Maine, 527 U.S. 706, 2248 (1999). Consequently, all the Articles of the Constitution could arguably be seen as altering the restrictions of the state sovereign immunity.

Another argument made by the Court in Seminole is that the Fourteenth Amendment was designed to alter the preexisting balance between state and federal power at the time of its passage. This argument is more plausible, but is still difficult to differentiate between Congress's power under the Fourteenth Amendment and Congress's power under the Articles of the Constitution. Like the Fourteenth Amendment, the Articles of the Constitution were clearly intended to alter the balance between state and federal power at the time of the passage of the Constitution, which included state sovereign immunity. This is exemplified by the Supremacy Clause, U.S. Const., Art. VI, cl. 2 which provides that laws passed under the Articles of the Constitution would be supreme over state law.

[131] 527 U.S. 706 (1999).

[132] 535 U.S. 743 (2002).

[133] 46 U.S.C. App. §1701 (1994 & Supp. V).

[134] 535 U.S. 760.

[135] The Court noted that "[there are] numerous common features shared by administrative adjudications and judicial proceedings." 535 U.S. at 756. "[F]ederal administrative law requires that agency adjudication contain many of the same safeguards as are available in the judicial process. The proceedings are adversary in nature. They are conducted before a trier of fact insulated from political influence. A party is entitled to present his case by oral or documentary evidence, and the transcript of testimony and exhibits together with the pleadings constitutes the exclusive record for decision. The parties are entitled to know the findings and conclusions on all of the issues of fact, law, or discretion presented on the record." Id.

[136] Justice Breyer noted that after this decision "a private person cannot bring a complaint against a State to a federal administrative agency where the agency (1) will use an internal adjudicative process to decide if the complaint is well founded, and (2) if so, proceed to court to enforce the law." Id. at 772.

[137] Id.

[138] For instance, the federal government has, in some cases, made the application of federal regulatory authority contingent, so that if a state chooses to regulate in that field, the federal regulatory role is circumscribed. In many cases, this will encourage states to regulate, so that the state has closer control of the application of such regulation within the state. See, e.g., 42 U.S.C. §7410 (national air control standards not applicable upon the adoption by states of adequate air control standards).

[139] 483 U.S. 203 (1987).

[140] 23 U.S.C. §158.

[141] U.S. Const., Art I, 8, cl 1 (Congress has the power to "lay and collect Taxes, Duties, Imposts, and Excises, to pay the Debts and provide for the common Defence and general Welfare of the United States").

[142] New York v. United States, 505 U.S. 144 (1992).

[143] Printz v. United States, 521 U.S. 898 (1997).

[144] It would seem that sovereign immunity is a core state power, and that requiring its waiver would raise Tenth Amendment concerns. See, e.g., National League of Cities v. Usery, 426

U.S. 833 (1976)(striking down federal wage and price controls on state employees as involving the regulation of traditional state functions). As discussed previously, however, the Court has, for the time being, abandoned this line of cases. Garcia v. San Antonio Metropolitan Transit Authority, 469 U.S. 528 (1985)(concluding that the test to identify traditional governmental functions had proven impractical, and that such disputes should be resolved through the political process).

[145] 483 U.S. at 207.

[146] Id. at 211.

[147] 132 S. Ct. 2566 (2012).

[148] P.L. 111-148.

[149] In NFIB, seven Justices held that the requirement that states either comply with the requirements of the Medicaid expansion under the ACA or lose all Medicaid funds violated the Tenth Amendment. However, these seven Justices either wrote or joined one of two separate opinions on this issue, and did not join in either the reasoning or judgment of the other opinion. The opinion of Chief Justice Roberts, which was joined by Justices Breyer and Kagan, appears to be significantly narrower than the dissenting opinion authored by Justices Scalia, Kennedy, Thomas, and Alito, and is thus controlling. Marks v. United States, 430 U.S. 188, 193 (1977)("[w]hen a fragmented Court decides a case and no single rationale explaining the result enjoys the assent of five Justices, 'the holding of the Court may be viewed as that position taken by those Members who concurred in the judgments on the narrowest grounds'") (citation omitted).

[150] The Court went on to hold, however, that the remedy was to sever that enforcement mechanism, effectively making state participation in the Medicaid expansion voluntary. 132 S. Ct. at 2607.

[151] For an analysis of the relationship between the Dole and NFIB case, see CRS Report R42367, Medicaid and Federal Grant Conditions After NFIB v. Sebelius: Constitutional Issues and Analysis, by Kenneth R. Thomas.

[152] 132 S. Ct. at 2604-05.

In: Separation of Powers …
Editor: Josephine Spencer

ISBN: 978-1-63485-189-3

Chapter 3

Testimony of Matthew Spalding, Associate Vice President and Dean of Educational Programs, Hillsdale College. Hearing on "The Original Understanding of the Role of Congress and How Far We've Drifted From It"*

The Rule of Law

The general concept of the rule of law—that government as well as the governed are subject to the law as promulgated and that all are to be equally protected by the law—long predates the founding of the United States. Its roots can be traced to classical antiquity where the most celebrated political philosophers sought to distinguish the rule of law from that of individual rulers or an oligarchic few. In the works of Plato and as developed in Aristotle's writings, the rule of law implies obedience to positive law as well as rudimentary checks on rulers and magistrates.

The rule of law has four key components. First, the rule of law means a formal, regular process of law enforcement and adjudication. What we really mean by "a government of laws, not of men" is the rule of men bound by law, not

* This is an edited, reformatted and augmented version of testimony presented March 1, 2016 before the House Judiciary Committee, Task Force on Executive Overreach.

subject to the arbitrary will of others. The rule of law means general rules of law that bind all people and are promulgated and enforced by a system of courts and law enforcement, not by mere discretionary authority. As James Madison writes in *Federalist* 62, speaking of Congress: "It will be of little avail to the people, that the laws are made by men of their own choice, if the laws be so voluminous that they cannot be read, or so incoherent that they cannot be understood; if they be repealed or revised before they are promulgated, or undergo such incessant changes that no man, who knows what the law is today, can guess what it will be to-morrow." In order to secure equal rights to all citizens, government must apply law fairly and equally through this legal process. Notice, hearings, indictment, trial by jury, legal counsel, the right against self-incrimination—these are all part of a fair and equitable "due process of law" that provides regular procedural protections and safeguards against abuse by government authority. Among the complaints lodged against the king in the Declaration of Independence was that he had "obstructed the administration of justice, by refusing his assent to laws for establishing judiciary powers," and was "depriving us in many cases, of the benefits of trial by jury."

Second, the rule of law means that these rules must be binding on rulers and the ruled alike. If the American people, Madison writes in *Federalist* 57, "shall ever be so far debased as to tolerate a law not obligatory on the legislature, as well as on the people, the people will be prepared to tolerate any thing but liberty." As all are subject to the law, so all—government and citizens, indeed all persons—are equal before the law, and equally subject to the legal system and its decisions. No one is above the law in respect to enforcement; no one is privileged to ignore the law, just as no one is outside the law in terms of its protection. As the phrase goes, all are presumed innocent until *proven* guilty. We see this equal application of equal laws reflected in the Constitution's references to "citizens" and "persons" rather than race, class, or some other group distinction, as in the Fifth Amendment's language that "[n]o person shall . . . be deprived of life, liberty, or property, without due process of law." It appears again in the Fourteenth Amendment's guarantee that "[n]o State shall . . . deny to any person within its jurisdiction the equal protection of the laws." The rights of all are dependent on the rights of each being defended and protected. In this sense, the rule of law is an expression of— indeed, is a requirement of—the idea of each person possessing equal rights.

Third, the rule of law implies that there are certain unwritten rules or generally understood standards to which specific laws and lawmaking must conform. There are some things that no government legitimately based on the rule of law can do. Many of these particulars were developed over the course of the history of

British constitutionalism, but they may be said to stem logically from the nature of law itself. Several examples can be seen in the clauses of the U.S. Constitution. There can be no "ex post facto" laws—that is, laws that classify an act as a crime leading to punishment after the act occurs. Nor can there be "bills of attainder," which are laws that punish individuals or groups without a judicial trial. We have already mentioned the requirement of "due process," but consider also the great writ of "habeas corpus" (no person may be imprisoned without legal cause) and the rule against "double jeopardy" (no person can be tried or punished twice for the same crime.) Strictly speaking, none of these rules are formal laws but follow from the nature of the rule of law. "Bills of attainder, ex-post facto laws and laws impairing the obligation of contracts," Madison writes in *Federalist* 44, "are contrary to the first principles of the social compact, and to every principle of sound legislation."

Lastly, even though much of its operation is the work of courts and judges, the rule of law is based on the absolute centrality of *lawmaking*. "The great end of men's entering into society, being the enjoyment of their properties in peace and safety, and the great instrument and means of that being the laws established in that society," writes John Locke in his *Second Treatise on Government*, "the first and fundamental positive law of all commonwealths is the establishing of the legislative power." Locke continues:

> This legislative is not only the supreme power of the commonwealth, but sacred and unalterable in the hands where the community have once placed it; nor can any edict of any body else, in what form soever conceived, or by what power soever backed, have the force and obligation of a law, which has not its sanction from that legislative which the public has chosen and appointed: for without this the law could not have that, which is absolutely necessary to its being a law, the consent of the society, over whom no body can have a power to make laws, but by their own consent, and by authority received from them. (Sec. 134)

Locke concludes that the bounds set upon the legislative power in all forms of government, stemming from consent and "the law of God and nature" are to govern by promulgated, established laws, not to raise taxes in particular without the consent of the people (recall the American rallying cry of 'no taxation without representation'), that laws are to be designed for no other end but the good of the people, and that the legislature "neither must nor can transfer the Power of making Laws to any body else, or place it anywhere but where the people have." Locke makes this last point clear:

> The legislative cannot transfer the power of making laws to any other hands: for it being but a delegated power from the people, they who have it cannot pass it over to others. The people alone can appoint the form of the common-wealth, which is by constituting the legislative, and appointing in whose hands that shall be. And when the people have said, We will submit to rules, and be governed by laws made by such men, and in such forms, no body else can say other men shall make laws for them; nor can the people be bound by any laws, but such as are enacted by those whom they have chosen, and authorized to make laws for them. The power of the legislative, being derived from the people by a positive voluntary grant and institution, can be no other than what that positive grant conveyed, which being only to make laws, and not to make legislators, the legislative can have no power to transfer their authority of making laws, and place it in other hands. (Sec. 141)

Lawmaking and the American Founding

The full implications of the constitutional development of the rule of law first appear in the principles and institutions of the American Founding. Virtually every government at the time was based on a claim to rule without popular consent. But the American Founders sought to break free of the old despotisms, characterized by the arbitrary will of the stronger, and to establish the rule of law and limited constitutional government based on consent. They held that man, though fallible and full of passions, is capable of governing himself and that none was so much better than another as to rule him without his consent.

The key turn in constitutional thinking came with the formal recognition that the inalienable rights belonging to each person by "the Laws of Nature and Nature's God" form the moral ground of government. For well over a century prior to the revolution, Americans had developed and become accustomed to the idea that governments are legitimately created only through fundamental agreement authorized by popular consent. The concept can be seen in the Massachusetts Constitution of 1780, which declares: "The body politic is formed by a voluntary association of individuals; it is a social compact by which the whole people covenants with each citizen and each citizen with the whole people." But it is summarized very simply in the words of the Declaration of Independence, which posits as a self-evident truth "that to secure these rights,

Governments are instituted among Men, deriving their just powers from the consent of the governed."

In addition to the initial formation of government, consent also gives guidance concerning the processes by which legitimate government operates. Among the charges lodged against the king in the Declaration of Independence is that he assented to Parliament's "imposing Taxes on us without our Consent" and "has kept among us, in times of peace, Standing Armies without the Consent of our legislatures." Indeed, the first six charges against the king address interference with local legislation and legislatures, violating "the right of Representation in the Legislature, a right inestimable to them and formidable to tyrants only." Consent does not necessarily mean pure democratic rule, but it does require a process of popular agreement to lawmaking and governance. In America, this was understood to mean a popular form of representative government. Only a government that derived its power from "the great body of the people," according to *Federalist* 39, was compatible with the "genius of the American people," "the fundamental principles of the revolution," and a determination to "rest all our political experiments on the capacity of mankind for self-government."

The Importance of Article I

The Constitution establishes three branches of government of equal rank in relation to each other. These branches are separated in accordance with the distinct powers, duties, and responsibilities stemming from the primary functions of governing: to make laws, to execute and enforce the laws, and to uphold (judge or adjudicate) the rule of those laws by applying them to particular individuals or cases. No branch is higher or lower than any other, and no branch controls the others. Each is vested with independent authority and unique powers that cannot be given away or delegated to others.

The order in which these branches are treated in the Constitution– legislature, executive, judiciary – is itself important. It moves from the most to the least "democratic" and from the most to the least directly chosen by the people. The members of the legislature "are distributed and dwell among the people at large," writes Madison in *Federalist* 50. "Their connections of blood, of friendship, and of acquaintance embrace a great proportion of the most influential part of the society. The nature of their public trust implies a personal influence among the people, and that they are more immediately the confidential guardians of the rights and liberties of the people." The Constitution lodges the basic power of government in the legislature not only because it is the branch most directly representative of popular consent but also because the very essence of governing according to the rule of law is centered on the legitimate authority to make laws.

Article I begins: “All legislative powers herein granted shall be vested in a Congress of the United States, which shall consist of a Senate and House of Representatives.” This language implies that while there might be other legislative powers, Congress is granted all those “herein” recognized, meaning listed in various clauses of the Constitution. The legislative power includes seventeen topics listed in Article I, Section 8: taxing and borrowing, interstate and foreign commerce, naturalization and bankruptcy, currency and counterfeiting, post offices and post roads, patents and copyrights, federal courts, piracy, the military, and the governance of the national capitol and certain federal enclaves. All told, the powers are not extensive, but they are vital. Apart from some relatively minor matters, the Constitution added to the authority already granted in the Articles of Confederation only the powers to regulate foreign and interstate commerce and to apportion “direct” taxes among the states according to population.

The diverse powers granted to Congress might at first seem rather disorganized, ranging from the clearly momentous (to declare war) to the seemingly minute (to fix weights and measures). But upon reflection, an underlying pattern emerges based on the distinction between key functions assigned to the national government and those left to the state governments. The two most important functions concern the nation’s security (such as the powers to maintain national defense) and the national economy (such as the power to tax or to regulate interstate commerce). And as might be expected, many of the powers complement each other in supporting those functions: The power to regulate interstate commerce, for instance, is consistent with the power to control currency, which is supported in turn by the power to punish counterfeiting and to establish standards for weights and measures.

Of utmost significance is Congress’ “power of the purse.” The source of Congress's power to spend derives from Article I, Section 8, Clause 1. The Appropriations Clause, though, makes Congress the final arbiter of the use of public funds and gives it a mechanism to control or to limit spending by the federal government. The language here is of limitation, not authorization (No Money shall be drawn from the Treasury, but in Consequence of Appropriations made by Law...) and it is placed in Section 9 of Article I, along with other restrictions on governmental actions to limit, most notably, executive action.

While the federal government’s powers are limited, the powers granted to it are complete. The Founders sought to create an energetic government with all powers needed to do the jobs assigned to it. Consequently, the enumerated powers of the federal government are supported by the auxiliary authority needed to carry out these functions. The central example of this is the "necessary and proper" clause, which empowers Congress to "make all Laws which shall be necessary and proper for carrying into Execution the foregoing Powers, and all other Powers vested by this Constitution in the Government of the United States, or in any Department or Officer thereof." While this language suggests a wide sweep of "implied" powers, it is not a grant to do anything and everything, but only to make those additional laws that are necessary and proper for execution of the powers expressed in the Constitution.

To further limit the expansion of legislative power and to prevent the legislature from intruding upon the powers of the other branches, Article I divides Congress into two chambers (bicameralism) chosen by two different political constituencies and with different terms of office: the House of Representatives, each member being elected by districts every two years, and the Senate, with members (originally) appointed by state legislatures to serve staggered terms of six years each. The House is based on popular representation, and the Senate on equal representation of all of the states. Unlike the House, which is intended to be responsive to the ebb and flow of popular opinion (which is why revenue bills originate in the House), the Senate—with its longer terms of office and a larger and distinct constituency—was to be more stable, deliberative, and oriented toward long-term state and national concerns. It is because of the nature of the Senate that the chamber is given unique responsibilities concerning the approval of executive appointments (for judges, ambassadors, and all other officers of the United States) and treaties with other countries.

The Separation of Powers

"In framing a government which is to be administered by men over men, the great difficulty lies in this," Madison writes in *Federalist* 51. "You must first enable the government to control the governed; and in the next place oblige it to controul itself." That meant that, in addition to performing its proper constitutional functions (lawmaking, executing and adjudicating the law), there needed to be an internal check to further limit the powers of government. Rather than create another coercive authority for that purpose (a dubious proposition to say the least), the Founders not only divided power but also set it against itself. This separation of powers, along with the further provisions for checks and balances, is the defining structural mechanism of the Constitution and creates a dynamism within the workings of government that uses the interests and incentives of those in government to enforce constitutional limits beyond their mere statement. It divides the powers of government among three branches and vests each with independent powers and responsibilities. Each has its own basis of authority and serves different terms of office. No member of one branch can at the same time serve in another branch.

Preserving the separation of powers was hardly a trifling concern for the Founders. Keeping the powers of government divided among distinct branches is "admitted on all hands to be essential to the preservation of liberty," Madison notes in *Federalist* 47. Here the founders were following the writings of Montesquieu, who made a strong case for such a division. "The accumulation of all powers," Madison continues, "legislative, executive, and judiciary, in the same hands, whether of one, a few, or many, and whether hereditary, self-appointed, or elective, may justly be pronounced the very definition of tyranny." For this reason, each branch has only those powers granted to it, and can do only what its particular grant of power authorizes it to do.

But it was not enough merely to define the powers of each branch and hope that they remained nicely confined within the written barriers of the Constitution. The Founders were acutely aware that each branch of government would be tempted to encroach upon the powers of the other. This was especially the case with the legislature: The "parchment barriers" of early state constitutions had proven an inadequate defense against a legislative proclivity toward "everywhere extending the sphere of its activity and drawing all power into its impetuous vortex." (*Federalist* 48) It is with this proclivity in mind that the Founders sought to grant each branch of government the means to preserve its rightful powers from encroachments by the others.

The solution is found in structuring government such that "its several constituent parts may, by their mutual relations, be the means of keeping each other in their proper places," as Madison explaines in *Federalist* 51. In other words, government is structured so that each branch has an interest in keeping an eye on the others, checking powers while jealously protecting its own. By giving each department an incentive to check the other—with overlapping functions and contending ambitions—the Founders devised a system that recognized and took advantage of man's natural political motivations to both use power for the common good and to keep power within constitutional boundaries. Or as Madison put it, the "interest of the man [becomes] connected with the constitutional rights of the place."

To this end, each branch of government shares overlapping powers with the others. Before it becomes law, for instance, congressional legislation must be approved by the executive—who also has a check against Congress in the form of the qualified veto, which the legislature in turn can override by two-thirds votes in the House and the Senate. The president is commander in chief but the House has the power to declare war, and it is up to Congress to fund executive activities, including war-making. Treaties and judicial appointments are made by the executive but only with the advice and consent of the Senate. The Supreme Court can strike down executive or legislative actions that come up in cases before it as unconstitutional, but Congress has the power to reenact or modify overturned laws, strip the court's jurisdiction in many cases, and impeach federal judges. As Joseph Story writes in his *Commentaries on the Constitution of the United States*, because power is of "an encroaching nature" it ought to be effectually restrained from passing the limits assigned to it so that while sharing power none should have an "overruling influence" in the operation of another branch's powers.

The separation of powers and the introduction of legislative balances and checks, according to Hamilton in *Federalist* 9, are "means, and powerful means, by which the excellencies of republican government may be retained and its imperfections lessened or avoided." They discourage the concentration of power and frustrate tyranny. At the same time, they require the branches of government to collaborate and cooperate in doing their work, limiting conflict and strengthening consensus. But these means also have the powerful effect of focusing individual actors on protecting their constitutional powers and carrying out their constitutional duties and functions—and that fact transforms the separation of powers from a mere negative concept to a positive and important contributor to limited government and constitutional fidelity.

Today, the separation of powers is often faulted for encouraging "gridlock." The Founders, however, understood the need for the good administration of government — an important aspect of their "improved science of politics." But they also understood that the administration of things was subordinate to the laws of Congress, and thus responsible to the people through election. As Alexander Hamilton points out in *Federalist* 68, it is a "heresy" to suggest that of all forms of government "that which is best administered is best." In the end, liberty is assured not by the anarchy of no government, on the one hand, or the arbitrary rule of unlimited government, on the other, but through a carefully designed and maintained structure of government to secure rights and prevent tyranny through the rule of law.

The New Science of Politics

The concept of the modern state and its "new science of politics" can be traced to the likes of the French philosophes and continental utopians of the 18th century who were deeply enamored with the endless promises of reason and modern science to solve all aspects of the human condition. Just as science brought technological changes and new methods of study to the physical world, so it would bring great change and continuous improvement to society and man. The late-19th-century, so-called "Progressives" took this argument, combined it with ideas from German idealism and historicism, and Americanized it to reshape the old constitutional rule of law model—which was seen as obsolete, inefficient, and designed to stifle change—into a new, more efficient form of democratic government. Their view of scientific rationalism questioned the very idea of self-governing citizenship: Liberty, they asserted, is not, as understood by the Founders, a condition consistent with human nature and the exercise of God-given natural rights, but an evolving concept to be socially constructed.

While seeming to advocate more democracy, the first progressives — under a Republican president, Theodore Roosevelt, and then a Democratic one, Woodrow Wilson — pursued the opposite when it came to government action. "All that progressives ask or desire," Wilson wrote in 1912, "is permission — in an era when 'development,' 'evolution,' is the scientific word — to interpret the Constitution according to the Darwinian principle; all they ask is recognition of the fact that a nation is a living thing and not a machine." To encourage democratic change while directing and controlling it, progressives posited a sharp distinction between politics and what they called "administration." Politics would remain the realm of expressing opinions – hence the continued relevance of Congress to provide rough guidelines – but the real decisions and details of governing would be handled by administrators, separate and supposedly immune from the influence of politics.

These administrators would be in charge of running a new form of government, designed to keep up with the ever-expanding aims of government, called "the administrative state." Where the Founders went to great lengths to preserve consent and limit government through republican institutions and the separation of powers, the progressives held that the barriers erected by the Founders had to be removed or circumvented so as to unify and expand the powers of government and to direct its actions toward achieving more and more progress and social change.

The particulars of accomplishing the broad objectives of reform—the details of regulation and many rule-making functions previously left to legislatures—were to be given over to a new class of professionals who would reside in the recesses of agencies like the FCC (Federal Communications Commission), the SEC (Securities and Exchange Commission), the CPSC (Consumer Product Safety Commission), or OSHA (Occupational Safety and Health Administration). As "objective" and "neutral" experts, so the theory went, these administrators would act above petty partisanship and faction, making decisions mostly unseen and beyond public scrutiny to accomplish the broad objectives of policy reform. The term "bureaucracy" comes from the French for desk, and the Greek for rule. The word was originally satirical, but for the progressives, the rule of clerks is a noble endeavor — they are the true "agents of democracy," as the progressive writer Herbert Croly put it.

The constantly changing structure of the administrative state requires dynamic management to keep it moving forward, of course, and so the new thinkers developed their own concept of "leadership" to complete their theory of government. If the times are constantly changing, and if the constitutional system must always evolve to adapt to that change, there must be a role for those who have the foresight and ability to lead the nation in the new directions of history, keeping ahead of popular opinion and always pointing the nation toward its future development. This clarity of vision and unity of direction—of rhetorical inspiration combined with strong political management—is to be provided especially by vigorous presidential leadership. In this new conception of the state, government is administrative and bureaucratic, subject only to the perceived wants of the popular will, under the forward-looking guidance of progressive leadership. In this view, government must always evolve and expand, and be ever more actively involved in day-to-day American life. Given the unlimited goal, government by definition must itself be unlimited. How could there be any limit? "It is denied that any limit can be set to governmental activity," wrote the progressive political scientist Charles Merriam.

> The exigencies of modern industrial and urban life have forced the state to intervene at so many points where an immediate individual interest is difficult to show, that the old doctrine has been given up for the theory that the state acts for the general welfare. It is not admitted that

> there are no limits to the action of the state, but on the other hand it is fully conceded that there are no natural rights which bar the way. The question is now one of expediency rather than of principle.

There was no longer any principle—whether natural rights or constitutional government derived from those rights—that limited the action of the state.

The Rise of Central Administration

The United States has been moving down the path of administrative government in fits and starts for some time, from the initial Progressive Era reforms through the New Deal's interventions in the economy. But the most significant shift and expansion occurred more recently, under the Great Society and its progeny. Progressives had initially sought to regulate certain targeted commercial activity such as railroads, trucking, aviation, and banking. But when the federal government assumed responsibility for the well-being of every American, it set about creating programs (and reforming old ones) to manage the whole range of socioeconomic policy, from employment, civil rights, welfare, and healthcare to the environment and elections. The expansion of regulatory activities on a society-wide scale in the 1960s and 1970s led to vast new centralizing authority in the federal government and a vast expansion of federal regulatory authority. This centralization of power brought with it what we conventionally mean by big government: huge workforces, massive expenditures, and extensive debt.

When administration is nationalized, though, it does not easily or naturally fall under the authority of one branch or another. As four decades of political history show, bureaucracy and its control created a new source of conflict between the executive and legislative branches. During the first part of our bureaucratic history, Congress had the upper hand, with presidents (at least since Richard Nixon) trying as they could to control the Fourth Branch. Congress, after all, had been creating these regulatory agencies to carry out its wishes and delegating its legislative powers to them in the form of broad regulatory authority. Congress was the first to adapt to the administrative state, continuously reorganizing itself since 1970 by committees and subcommittees to oversee and interact with the day-to-day operations of the bureaucratic apparatus. As the bureaucracy expanded, Congress sought to develop additional powers over the administrative state, the best-known of which was the legislative veto, held unconstitutional by the Supreme Court in

1983. Rather than control or diminish the bureaucracy through lawmaking or budget control, Congress has settled mostly on oversight of and providing "regulatory relief" from the bureaucracy.

Today, the primary function of modern government is to regulate. When Congress writes legislation, it uses very broad language that turns extensive power over to agencies, which are also given the authority of executing and usually adjudicating violations of their regulations in particular cases. The result is that most of the actual decisions of lawmaking and public policy— decisions previously the constitutional responsibility of elected legislators—are delegated to bureaucrats whose "rules" there is no doubt have the full force and effect of laws passed by Congress. In 2014, Congress passed and the President signed about 220 pieces of legislation in to law, amounting to a little over 3,000 pages of law, while federal departments and agencies issued 79,066 pages of new and updated regulations. The modern Congress is almost exclusively a supervisory body exercising post-legislative oversight of administrative policymakers.

Modern administrative forms of governing consolidate the powers of government by exercising the lawmaking power, executing their own rules and then judging their application in administrative courts, binding individuals not through legislative law or judicial decision but through case-by-case rulemaking based on increasingly broad and undefined mandates, with more and more authority over an ever wider range of subjects, all the while less and less apparent and accountable to the political process and popular consent. The problem with such arbitrary, comprehensive, unchecked power is that it is not administration at all but rule outside of the law, outside of the Constitution and its checks and balances, and outside of (and thus not responsive to) our democratic institutions of government.

The consequences of the administrative state's lack of accountability have been made much more severe by Congress's current inclination to deal with every policy issue through comprehensive legislation. Congress has ceased to tackle distinct problems with simple laws that can be deliberated upon and then made known to the public. Instead, for everything from financial restructuring to environmental regulation to immigration reform, Congress proposes labyrinth bills that that extend to every corner of civil society and impose an ever more complicated and expansive administrative apparatus upon a public that increasingly has no time or means to understand the laws it will be held accountable for. The Affordable Care Act is a perfect example. This law passed by Congress transferred massive regulatory authority over one-sixth of the American economy, not to mention over most health-care decisionmaking, to a collection of more than 100 federal agencies, bureaus, and commissions, along with new federal programs and an unprecedented delegation of power to the Secretary of Health and Human Services. Little or nothing will be allowed outside the new regulatory scheme — no alternative state programs, no individuals or businesses that choose not to participate, no truly private market alternatives. Likewise, the Dodd-Frank Wall Street Reform and Consumer Protection Act. Its 2,300 pages require administrative rule-makings reaching not only to every financial institution but well in to every corner of the American economy. Its new bureaucracies, like the Consumer Financial Protection Bureau and the Financial Stability Oversight Council, operate outside of the public eye and are subject to virtually none of the traditional checks. The CFPB is literally outside the rule of law: it has an independent source of revenue, insulation from legislative or executive oversight, and the broad latitude and discretion to determine and enforce its own rulings—as so define the limits of its own authority—based on vague terms left undefined.

The rise of the new imperial presidency—acting by executive orders more than legislative direction—should come as no surprise given the overwhelming amount of authority that has been delegated to decision-making actors and bodies largely under executive control. As Congress has expanded the bureaucracy—creating innumerable agencies, delegating its lawmaking authority, neglecting control of the details of budgeting, and focusing on ex post facto checks—the executive has attained unprecedented levels of authority. Modern executives can command the bureaucracy to implement new policies without the cooperation of Congress by abusing executive discretion, by exploiting the vagaries of poorly written laws, and by willfully neglecting and disregarding even those laws which are clear and well-crafted. By acting unilaterally without or against the authority of Congress, the executive not only assumes a degree of legislative powers without legislative accountability but also avoids responsibility for executing the laws legitimately authorized by Congress. The next president— regardless of political party—will be sorely tempted and under significant pressure to achieve desired policy goals by following the precedent of prior administrations that ignored the will of Congress and the text of existing laws. Once it has been established that the president can govern by executive orders and regulations without Congress, and by extension the law itself, it will prove difficult and perhaps impossible to prevent future executives from following this lawless path.

Rebuilding Congress

It may be a prudent option, especially in the face of today's pen-and-phone presidency, to assert checks and balances through litigation. There is, no doubt, something qualitatively different in how this president is using (and abusing) his powers, with and without congressional authorization. At the very least, a successful lawsuit could prevent things from getting worse. But this much is clear: the legislative branch going to the judicial branch to solve its disagreements with the executive branch is not going to solve the problem. If Congress' turning to litigation to assert its constitutional prerogative becomes the norm, it would have the perverse (and unintended) effect of further nullifying the institutional powers of Congress.

The only way to reverse the trend of a diminishing legislature and the continued expansion of the bureaucratic executive is for Congress to strengthen its constitutional muscles as a coequal branch of government in our separation of powers system. This is the solution envisioned by our Founders, and consistent with popular consent. A stronger legislative branch would go a long way toward making the role of government a proper political question, as it should be, subject to election rather than executive fiat or judicial decree.

The Constitution is grounded in the principle that governments derive their just powers from the consent of the governed. This means that laws must be made by the representatives elected by the people and not unelected bureaucrats. Thus the first step towards restoring the structural integrity of the Constitution is for Congress to reassert its legislative authority and, as much as possible, to cease delegating what amounts to the power to make laws to bureaucrats and administrative agencies. In any case where it allows administrators the discretion to create significant rules, Congress should assert its authority to approve or reject those rules.

Congress needs to relearn the art of lawmaking. It must regain legislative control over today's labyrinthine state, bringing consent and responsibility back to government through better lawmaking up front and, as a result, better oversight after the fact. Regular legislative order, especially the day-to-day back-and-forth of authorizing, appropriating and overseeing the operations of government, will do more than anything to restore the Article I powers of Congress and return legislative control over today's unlimited government.

And the one place where the power of Congress is not entirely lost—and where there is opportunity for gaining leverage over an unchecked executive – is Congress' power of the purse. Used well, it will also prevent Congress from continually getting cornered in time sensitive fights over messy and incomprehensible omnibus budgets at the end of every year, the settlement of which works to the advantage of the executive. Strategically controlling and using the budget process will turn the advantage back to Congress, forcing the executive to engage with the legislative branch and get back into the habit of executing the laws enacted by Congress—no more and no less.

If Congress does not act to correct the growing tilt toward executive-bureaucratic power, the structure of our government will be fundamentally, and perhaps permanently, altered. This imperils the constitutional design and great achievement of republican government. It is still possible for Congress to restore its legislative powers, and to correct this structural imbalance. But Congress needs to think strategically and act as a constitutional institution – indeed, the primary branch of constitutional government. And it must begin doing so now, forcefully stating its argument, putting down clear markers and drawing enforceable institutional lines before the inauguration of the next president—whoever they may be, and regardless of their political party.

Thank you.

In: Separation of Powers …
Editor: Josephine Spencer
ISBN: 978-1-63485-189-3

Chapter 4

TESTIMONY OF STEPHEN I. VLADECK, PROFESSOR OF LAW, AMERICAN UNIVERSITY, WASHINGTON COLLEGE OF LAW. HEARING ON "THE ORIGINAL UNDERSTANDING OF THE ROLE OF CONGRESS AND HOW FAR WE'VE DRIFTED FROM IT"*

Chairman King, Ranking Member Cohen, and distinguished members of the Task Force:

Thank you for inviting me to testify today on such a timely and important topic. Few structural relationships are more important in our constitutional system than the interplay between Congress and the Executive Branch, and I do not think there can be any doubt that there are reasons to fear for the contemporary and future health of this vital dynamic.

Where I suspect that I part company from my fellow witnesses, and from many Members of this Task Force, however, is in my assessment of the *causes* of the current breakdown in this relationship. Whereas many have been quick to place the blame on President Obama and the allegedly unfettered executive power he has repeatedly sought to wield throughout his Administration,[1] my own view is that the disease that currently plagues the separation of powers is

---

* This is an edited, reformatted and augmented version of testimony presented March 1, 2016 before the House Judiciary Committee, Task Force on Executive Overreach.

far more attributable to legislative torpor — an unwillingness on the part of Congress aggressively to police the authority previously delegated to the Executive Branch through substantive legislation.

In *Federalist 51*, James Madison famously explained that, for our system of separated powers to function, "Ambition must be made to counteract ambition."[2] I couldn't agree more. But to date, the 114th Congress has enacted *126* Public Laws[3] — fewer than half the total of the most unproductive Congress in American history, the 112th (which passed *283*).[4] By contrast, the 80th Congress (which President Truman famously derided as the "Do-Nothing Congress") enacted *906* public bills.[5] And beyond this quantitative assessment, the legislation that this Congress *has* enacted has said virtually nothing about health care, immigration, environmental regulation, or the war powers — some of the substantive policy areas in which the criticisms of the current Administration have been the loudest.

Reasonable minds can and will surely disagree about the *merits* of President Obama's policy ambitions in these areas (and others). What cannot be gainsaid is that this Congress has been uniquely reluctant to counteract or otherwise mitigate those ambitions through the conventional vehicle of substantive legislation. Thus, any contemporary drift from the original understanding, in my view, has been at least as much a result of congressional passivity as it has been a result of presidential aggressiveness.

The reason why this matters, as I explain in my testimony this morning, is because of the subtle but crucial distinction between two different types of executive power: *Indefeasible* (or "preclusive") power, pursuant to which the President claims the authority to ignore statutory constraints on his authority, and *defeasible* power, pursuant to which the President claims the authority to act unilaterally only in the face of congressional silence, and does *not* assert the authority to defy statutory prohibitions.

An overwhelming majority of the criticisms of the Obama administration of which I am aware fall into this latter category. Indeed, on a host of topics, the Administration has all-but disavowed any inclination to defy statutory constraints, such as the restrictions on the transfers of Guantánamo detainees into the United States.[6] Contrast that with, for example, the Bush administration, which repeatedly made claims of *indefeasible* power — the authority to ignore statutes that, among other things, prohibited torture;[7] limited the government's power to conduct warrantless surveillance;[8] required statutory authorization for the detention of U.S. citizens as "enemy combatants";[9] and so on.[10] A common refrain during the Bush administration was that statutes Congress enacted to limit the President's power were unconstitutional insofar as they succeeded in doing so. We've heard far less of that argument from the White House over the past seven years.

Once more, though, it is not my goal today to re-litigate the merits of the Bush administration's claims to indefeasible power. Rather, the relevant point for present purposes is that, when the Executive Branch claims indefeasible power, it is the courts that are in the best position to stop it. But when the Executive Branch claims only *defeasible* power, that power can (and historically has been) meaningfully circumscribed by Congress — through statutes imposing limits on such authority. Thus, at the end of the day, the best solution to the contemporary perception, valid or otherwise, that the President is overreaching through claims of defeasible executive power is, quite simply, new legislation more precisely delimiting his authority.

I

As Justice Robert Jackson famously explained in his concurrence in the *Steel Seizure* case,

> When the President takes measures incompatible with the expressed or implied will of Congress, his power is at its lowest ebb, for then he can rely only upon his own constitutional powers minus any constitutional powers of Congress over the matter. Courts can sustain exclusive Presidential control in such a case only be disabling the Congress from acting upon the subject. Presidential claim to a power at once so conclusive and preclusive must be scrutinized with caution, for what is at stake is the equilibrium established by our constitutional system.[11]

But where no statute specifically limits the President's authority, in contrast, "congressional inertia, indifference or quiescence may sometimes, at least as a practical matter, enable, if not invite, measures on independent presidential responsibility."[12]

Although Justice Jackson's concurrence is often celebrated as a canonical articulation of how we ought to assess the merits of separation-of-powers disputes between the political branches, one can find the very same understanding in one of the Supreme Court's first separation-of-powers cases, *Little* v. *Barreme*.[13] Because I believe it is reflective of the Founding-era understandings of the difference between defeasible and indefeasible executive power, it's worth laying out the decision's background in some detail:[14]

In response to escalating tension between the U.S. and French governments, largely a result of the 1794 Jay Treaty[15] with Great Britain and the "XYZ Affair,"[16] Congress in 1798 rescinded a series of 1778 treaties with France.[17] During the same session, it enacted the controversial Alien[18] and Sedition[19] Acts and the oft-neglected but still extant Alien Enemy Act.[20] The Fifth Congress also enacted statutes suspending commerce with France and otherwise providing for reprisals against French shipping for offenses against U.S. merchant ships.[21] President Adams did not request, nor did Congress provide, a declaration of war.[22] Thus, the Quasi-War was America's first experience with the concept of "undeclared" or "imperfect" war, where the scope of the conflict depended far more directly on the specific terms of the underlying statutory authorizations.[23]

Consequently, in the first Supreme Court case arising out of the conflict, *Bas* v. *Tingy*,[24] the issue was whether France was an "enemy" within the meaning of a 1799 Non-Intercourse Act[25] at the time that the cargo ship *Eliza* was captured by the *Ganges*, an armed U.S. vessel, notwithstanding the absence of a formal declaration of war by the United States Congress.[26] In seriatim opinions,[27] the Court concluded that France was in fact an "enemy," triggering the recovery provided for by the 1799 statute.

The second Supreme Court case stemming from the Quasi-War was *Talbot* v. *Seeman*,[28] which concerned the authority of the U.S. Navy to capture *neutral* vessels that the Navy had probable cause to believe were in fact French ships.[29] Although no Act of Congress expressly authorized such captures, Chief Justice Marshall, in his first published opinion, traced implicit authority for the capture to the language of several of the Fifth Congress's non-intercourse statutes, suggesting that such authority must come from congressional statutes, as opposed to inherent executive power.[30]

But by far the most important of the Quasi-War cases, at least for present purposes, was the last[31] of the trilogy—*Little*.[32] At issue in *Little* was the scope of a congressional non-intercourse statute, enacted on February 9, 1799, which empowered the President to authorize "the commanders of the public armed ships of the United States" to stop and search ships suspected of carrying French goods and to seize any such ship "bound or sailing *to* any port or place within the territory of the French Republic."[33] President Adams, through the Secretary of the Navy, subsequently issued instructions authorizing seizures of vessels "bound to *or* from" French ports.[34] As Professor Sidak has summarized:

Captain George Little commanded the U.S. frigate *Boston*. On December 2, 1799, the *Boston* captured *The Flying-Fish*, a Danish ship carrying Danish and neutral cargo, as it sailed from Jeremie to the Danish port of St. Thomas in the Virgin Islands. Little was acting under executive orders in enforcing the non-intercourse law that prohibited American vessels from journeying to French ports, a statute that Little suspected *The Flying-Fish* of violating. The district court ordered restoration of the ship and cargo, but declined to award damages for capture and detention. The circuit court reversed and awarded damages, on the rationale that the capture would have been unlawful even if *The Flying-Fish* had been an American vessel.[35]

Writing for a unanimous Court, Chief Justice Marshall affirmed, and held that Captain Little was liable for damages.[36] What commentators tend to overlook about Chief Justice Marshall's short but forceful opinion in *Little* is the extent to which he clearly understood the distinction between unilateral presidential power in the absence of congressional action and the scope of such authority in the face of countervailing congressional limitations, even — as in *Little* — potentially illogical ones.[37] That is, Marshall plainly suggested that the issue might be different had Congress not interposed ***any*** limits on the Navy's authority to capture suspected French ships, but that the existence of a limit rendered unlawful any seizures in violation thereof.[38] In his words,

> It is by no means clear that the president of the United States whose high duty it is to "take care that the laws be faithfully executed," and who is commander in chief of the armies and navies of the United States, might not, without any special authority for that purpose, in the then existing state of things, have empowered the officers commanding the armed vessels of the United States, to seize and send into port for adjudication, American vessels which were forfeited by being engaged in this illicit commerce. But when it is observed that . . . the 5th section [of the 1799 Non-Intercourse Act] gives a special authority to seize on the high seas, and ***limits*** that authority to the seizure of vessels bound or sailing ***to*** a French port, the legislature seems to have prescribed that the manner in which this law shall be carried into execution, was to exclude a seizure of any vessel ***not*** bound to a French port.[39]

In other words, whether or not President Adams could have issued the instructions at issue in the absence of a statutory constraint, the existence of the constraint settled the illegality of Captain Little's actions.

To be sure, I don't mean to make too much of *Little*. But (1) as the *Steel Seizure* case underscores, Marshall's original understanding of the distinction between defeasible and indefeasible presidential power has persisted in the Supreme Court's separation of powers jurisprudence; and (2) if anything, it was even more forcefully reiterated by the Supreme Court just a decade ago, when Justice Stevens emphasized that, "Whether or not the President has independent power, absent congressional authorization, to convene military commissions, he may not *disregard limitations* that Congress has, in proper exercise of its own war powers, placed on his powers."[40]

Of course, the President will still occasionally *prevail* in arguments that a substantive limitation imposed by Congress unconstitutionally interferes with his inherent constitutional authority; we need look no further than the Supreme Court's June 2015 decision in *Zivotofsky* v. *Kerry*[41] for evidence of that. And as noted above, the purpose of my testimony is not to rehash the well-joined debate over when Congress may and may not impose such restraints. My point today is far more modest: Until and unless Congress actually *does* impose such limits on the President's powers, any perceived separation-of-powers violation is, in my view, far less pernicious than in the context of an inappropriate claim of indefeasible power, where even the most unambiguous legislative mandates may go unenforced.

II

Lest my testimony today be taken as a defense of the Obama administration's actions on Article II grounds, however, let me also note another recurring feature of separation-of-powers debates that are portrayed in defeasibility terms: Oftentimes, the dispute is not, in fact, over whether the President has the inherent constitutional authority to act in the face of congressional silence, but rather whether the President is acting in good faith *pursuant to* the relevant statutory authorities.

As a case in point, consider the current debate over the President's legal authority to use military force against the Islamic State in Iraq and the Levant (ISIL). The Obama administration has consistently maintained, since September 2014, that outside the specific context of self-defense, its general authority to use such force derives not from Article II of the Constitution, but from a statute, *i.e.*, the September 2001 Authorization for the Use of Military Force[42] — even though that Act (1) says nothing at all about ISIL; and (2) only authorizes force against groups that were responsible for, or assisted in, the attacks of September 11 (which occurred before ISIL even existed).

Some agree with the Obama administration's legal reasoning; others do not. (In my view, the validity of the argument almost certainly turns upon factual details — about the origins of ISIL and its relationship with al Qaeda — that remain classified.[43]) Regardless, even if the Obama administration is *incorrect* in its interpretation of the AUMF, all that conclusion would mean is that the Executive Branch is incorrectly interpreting a statute — not that it is willfully abusing its inherent constitutional authority. The same goes for the Administration's Clean Power Plan, its implementation of the Affordable Care Act, and its deferred action immigration program, among others; the disputes in all of these contexts reduce to whether or not the Executive Branch's interpretation of vague (and, at times, inconsistent) statutory delegations is permissible. You and I may answer those questions differently, but as with any question of statutory interpretation, the ultimate authority is Congress — which can always pass legislation clarifying the meaning of the original text, whether before, after, or in lieu of judicial interpretations thereof.

This is exactly why I, among others (including President Obama, who has submitted proposed legislation[44]), have repeatedly called upon this Congress to pass a new AUMF for ISIL[45] — not because I am convinced that the Obama administration is acting *unlawfully* in using force under the 2001 AUMF, but because, from a separationof-powers perspective, "Congress's inaction in the face of a President's debatable claims presidential warmaking in the future."[46] Indeed, as I've written before,

> For Congress to be in session and to simply refuse to vote, one way or the other, on war powers the President is exercising (to a large degree openly), is for Congress to invite *future* presidents not just to engage in greater unilateral warmaking, but in greater unilateral action during wartime, writ large. It would be one thing if Congress wasn't acting because it was convinced the President would *veto* any legislation (thereby exposing Congress's institutional weakness). But here, the President has repeatedly suggested that he would welcome a bill, has drafted one of his own, and has supported drafts provided by various members.[47]

In those circumstances, I simply don't see the argument that the President is overreaching — or that, if he is, it isn't with Congress's knowing and willful acquiescence. And although my focus in my testimony today has been on how the war powers aspect of this conversation reflects my thesis, similar arguments can be made about the absence of legislation clarifying the scope of the President's authority in virtually all of the other substantive policy areas of contemporary controversy.

Finally, I realize that one response to my testimony today may be to simply suggest that President Obama would veto any legislation seeking to clarify or overturn his Administration's interpretations of existing authorities, which would render unrealistic any prospect of this Congress enacting such legislation. In my view, there are two separate — but equally compelling — rejoinders to such a response:

First, from a separation of powers perspective, legislation that the President vetoes over significantly substantial policy differences would be the system working exactly the way it's supposed to — and if the legislation were perceived as reasserting Congress's institutional role rather than simply staking out a partisan substantive policy position, there might well be sufficient votes to *override* such a veto. After all, American history is replete with presidential vetoes being overridden by bipartisan supermajorities in Congress. *Second*, and as importantly, as in the ISIL AUMF context, there is no guarantee that such a veto would be forthcoming. Indeed, during his tenure to date, President Obama has vetoed fewer bills (nine) than any two-term President since James Monroe.[48] That's hardly the mark of a President who refuses to acknowledge Congress's constitutional authority in cases in which it has actually been asserted.

If nothing else, more aggressive efforts from Congress to rein-in perceived excesses in executive power would present a far more conventional separation of powers debate than one in which Congress merely objects to such perceived excesses *without* doing anything to circumscribe them.

* * *

Thank you again for the opportunity to testify before the Task Force this morning. I look forward to your questions.

End Notes

[1] See, e.g., DAVID E. BERNSTEIN, LAWLESS: THE OBAMA ADMINISTRATION'S UNPRECEDENTED ASSAULT ON THE CONSTITUTION AND THE RULE OF LAW (2015).

[2] THE FEDERALIST No. 51, at 321–22 (Clinton Rossiter ed., 1961) (James Madison).

[3] See Public Laws, CONGRESS.GOV, https://www.congress.gov/public-laws/114th-congress (last visited Feb. 26, 2016).

[4] See Statistics and Historical Comparison, GOVTRACK.US, https://www.govtrack.us/congress/bills/statistics (last visited Feb. 26, 2016).

[5] See Résumé of Congressional Activity, Eightieth Congress, http://www.senate.gov /reference/resources/ pdf/80res.pdf (last visited Feb. 26, 2016).

[6] See Marty Lederman, The Insoluble Guantánamo Problem, JUST SECURITY, Nov. 13, 2015, https://www.justsecurity.org/27563/guantanamo-problem-remains-insoluble-part-three-executive-disregard-gtmorestrictions-solution/.

[7] See 18 U.S.C. §§ 2340–2340A (2006).

[8] See id. § 2511(2)(f).

[9] See id. § 4001(a).

[10] For links to the Administration's legal arguments on this front, see Stephen I. Vladeck, Congress, the Commander-in- Chief, and the Separation of Powers After Hamdan, 16 TRANSNAT'L L. & CONTEMP. PROBS. 933, 937 n.22 (2007). For an exhaustive rebuttal of such claims, see David J. Barron & Martin S. Lederman, The Commander in Chief at the Lowest Ebb (pts. 1–2), 121 HARV. L. REV. 689, 941 (2008).

[11] Youngstown Sheet & Tube Co. v. Sawyer, 343 U.S. 579, 637–38 (1952) (Jackson, J., concurring).

[12] Id. at 637.

[13] 6 U.S. (2 Cranch) 170 (1804).

[14] Much of the discussion that follows is derived from Vladeck, supra note 10, at 941–43.

[15] Treaty of Amity, Commerce, and Navigation, U.S.-Gr. Brit., Nov. 19, 1794, 8 Stat. 116.

[16] See ALBERT BOWMAN, THE STRUGGLE FOR NEUTRALITY: FRANCO-AMERICAN DIPLOMACY DURING THE FEDERALIST ERA 306-33 (1974).

[17] Act of July 7, 1798, ch. 67, 1 Stat. 578 .

[18] Act of June 25, 1798, ch. 58, 1 Stat. 570 (expired 1800).

[19] Act of July 14, 1798, ch. 74, 1 Stat. 596 (expired 1801).

[20] Act of July 6, 1798, ch. 66, 1 Stat. 577 (codified as amended at 50 U.S.C. §§ 21-24 (2000)).

[21] See, e.g., Act of June 13, 1798, ch. 53, 1 Stat. 565; Act of June 25, 1798, ch. 60, 1 Stat. 572; Act of June 28, 1798, ch. 62, 1 Stat. 574; Act of July 9, 1798, ch. 68, 1 Stat. 578; Act of July 16, 1798, ch. 88, 1 Stat. 611.

[22] See J. Gregory Sidak, The Quasi-War Cases—and Their Relevance to Whether "Letters of Marque and Reprisal" Constrain Presidential War Powers, 28 HARV. J.L. & PUB. POL'Y 465, 481 (2005).

[23] See id.

[24] Bas v. Tingy, 4 U.S. (4 Dall.) 37 (1800).

[25] See Act of Mar. 2, 1799, ch. 24, § 7, 1 Stat. 709, 716 (repealed 1800).

[26] See Bas, 4 U.S. at 37. For a summary of the background of this case, see Sidak, supra note 22, at 483-86.

[27] In Bas, separate opinions (reaching the same result) were filed by Justices Moore, Washington, Chase, and Paterson. See id. at 39-40 (Moore, J.); id. at 40-43 (Washington, J.); id. at 43-45 (Chase, J.); id. at 45-46 (Paterson, J.).

[28] Talbot v. Seeman, 5 U.S. (1 Cranch) 1 (1801).

[29] See Sidak, supra note 22, at 487-90 (summarizing the background to Talbot).

[30] See Talbot, 5 U.S. at 28.

[31] One curiosity concerning Little is the lengthy and heretofore unexplained (and unexplored) delay between when the case was argued—December 16 and 19, 1801—and when it was decided, February 27, 1804. Although the Supreme Court did not sit in 1802 per the terms of the 1802 Judiciary Act, Little, the only case argued at the December 1801 Term not decided during the same Term, was not handed down during the February 1803 Term (the Court's next sitting), either. See SUPREME COURT OF THE U.S., DATES OF SUPREME COURT DECISIONS AND ARGUMENTS: U.S. REPORTS, VOLUMES 2-107 (1791-1882), at 3-4 (2006), http://www.supremecourtus.gov/opinions/ datesof decisions.pdf.

[32] Little v. Barreme, 6 U.S. (2 Cranch) 170 (1804).

[33] Act of Feb. 9, 1799, ch. 2, § 5, 1 Stat. 613, 615 (expired 1800) (emphasis added).

[34] Bradford R. Clark, Separation of Powers as a Safeguard of Federalism, 79 TEX. L. REV. 1321, 1394 (2001) (discussing Little).

[35] Sidak, supra note not defined., at 490 (footnotes omitted).

[36] Little, 6 U.S. (2 Cranch) 170.

[37] See id. at 177-78.

[38] Id.

[39] Id. at 177–78 (emphases added; original emphases omitted).

[40] Hamdan v. Rumsfeld, 548 U.S. 557, 593 n.23 (2006).

[41] 135 S. Ct. 2076 (2015) (invalidating an Act of Congress that required the State Department to list "Jerusalem, Israel" as the place of birth on the passports of U.S. citizens born in Jerusalem, because it contravened the President's constitutional authority to take no position on whether Jerusalem is part of Israel).

[42] Pub. L. No. 107-40, 115 Stat. 224 (codified at 50 U.S.C. § 1541 note).

[43] See Steve Vladeck, ISIL as al Qaeda: Three Reactions, LAWFARE, Sept. 11, 2014, https://www.lawfareblog .com/isil-al-qaeda-three-reactions.

[44] See Joint Resolution, available at https://www.whitehouse.gov/sites/default/files/docs/aumf 02112015.pdf (last visited Feb. 26, 2016).

[45] See, e.g., Jack Goldsmith, Ryan Goodman, and Steve Vladeck, Five Principles That Should Govern Any U.S. Authorization of Force, WASH. POST, Nov. 14, 2014, at A21.

[46] Steve Vladeck, The Irresponsible Institutional Politics of an "Election Year," JUST SECURITY, Jan. 4, 2016, https://www.justsecurity.org/28629/irresponsible-institutional-politics-election-year/.

[47] Id.

[48] See Summary of Bills Vetoed, U.S. SENATE, http://www.senate.gov/reference/Legislation/ Vetoes/ vetoCounts.htm (last visited Feb. 26, 2016).

INDEX

P

R

S

T

U

V

W